Dissociation and the Dynamics of Personality

Dissociation and the Dynamics of Personality addresses the nature of personality in trauma-dissociation and proposes a dynamic understanding of persons that fundamentally challenges conventional views of the self and consciousness.

This important book provides a clear and coherent understanding of how childhood trauma can lead to a range of dissociative responses, addressing the fundamental issues underlying the controversy in this field. By recognising causal complexity and the dynamic convergence of biology and culture, Boag demonstrates the significance of trauma-dissociation for understanding personality and consciousness. Drawing upon both philosophy of mind and current psychiatric and neurobiological evidence, this book proposes a dynamic understanding of persons that fundamentally challenges the conventional view of the self and consciousness.

Dissociation and the Dynamics of Personality will be of interest to readers concerned with the trauma-dissociation controversy, including philosophers of mind and psychiatrists. It will also interest psychological practitioners and psychologists, as well as anyone concerned with the implications of the dissociative mind for understanding personality.

Simon Boag is Associate Professor in the School of Psychological Sciences at Macquarie University, Australia. He has published extensively on the topics of personality psychology and psychodynamic theory and is the author of *Metapsychology and the Foundations of Psychoanalysis* and *Freudian Repression, the Unconscious, and the Dynamics of Inhibition* (both Routledge).

Dissociation and the Dynamics of Personality

Trauma, Consciousness, and Culture

Simon Boag

Routledge
Taylor & Francis Group

LONDON AND NEW YORK

Designed cover image: Getty | Jupiterimages

First published 2025
by Routledge
4 Park Square, Milton Park, Abingdon, Oxon OX14 4RN

and by Routledge
605 Third Avenue, New York, NY 10158

Routledge is an imprint of the Taylor & Francis Group, an informa business

British Library Cataloguing-in-Publication Data
A catalogue record for this book is available from the British Library

ISBN: 9781032357362 (hbk)
ISBN: 9780367428976 (pbk)
ISBN: 9781003328254 (ebk)

DOI: 10.4324/9781003328254

Typeset in Times New Roman
by codeMantra

For Luna and Loki

Contents

Acknowledgements

The foundation for this book was written while undertaking an Alexander von Humboldt Foundation Research Fellowship in Berlin, Germany. I am extremely grateful to the Alexander von Humboldt Foundation for making this work possible. I am also extremely grateful to my hosts at the International Psychoanalytic University for providing me with the opportunity to undertake this Fellowship in Berlin. Thanks also to the charismatic city of Berlin for such a great experience.

I would also like to thank Professor Erik Reichle, the former Head of School of Psychological Sciences at Macquarie University, for always working to provide an excellent research environment, and for his ongoing support and encouragement of my work. Thanks also go to his encouraging and constructive feedback on this text.

Thanks also go to Professor Martin Dorahy for both his kind encouragement and for providing some very helpful critical feedback on this text. I regret not having a greater opportunity to incorporate all of his critical points and suggestions, but they were much appreciated.

Thanks also go to Routledge for their patience throughout this process. The COVID-19 pandemic enforced a hiatus in writing and I thank Routledge for their understanding and continuing support throughout.

Lastly, thanks to my long-suffering family for putting up with me writing on weekends and whilst away on holiday. I promise that the next family holiday will be a proper one.

Chapter 1

Introduction

Traumatising childhood events are associated with subsequent lifetime mental and physical health problems (Bailey & Brand, 2017; Hughes et al., 2017). Despite the importance of understanding how the young mind accommodates traumatic stress, there is considerable dispute with respect to the claim that trauma causes psychological dissociation. Dissociation here typically refers to "a lack of integration of psychological processes that normally should be integrated" (Cardeña & Gleaves, 2007, p. 474; cf. Spiegel et al., 2011). Nearly any aspect of psychobiological functioning can become dissociated, including consciousness, memory, affect, identity, and personality (Cardeña, 1994; Cardeña & Carlson, 2011; Şar, 2014).

Notwithstanding the long history of viewing psychopathology in terms of disordered or unnatural mental associations (e.g., see Hoeldtke, 1967), there is particular controversy concerning the relationship between traumatising events and dissociative amnesia and dissociative identity disorder (DID) (Cardeña & Gleaves, 2007; Dalenberg et al., 2012, 2014; Lilienfeld et al., 1999; Lynn et al., 2014; Lynn et al., 2019; Merckelbach, Devilly & Rassin, 2002). With dissociative (or psychogenic) amnesia, memories of traumatising events that would otherwise be remembered remain ostensibly incapable of recall, while with DID, the personality fragments into relatively autonomous identities with degrees of amnesia between them (American Psychiatric Association (APA), 2022). DID is taken to exemplify the dissociative disorders (Spiegel et al., 2013) and is apparent in the widely publicised case of Sybil (Shirley Ardell Mason). Sybil purportedly developed 16 distinct personalities in response to enduring childhood abuse inflicted by her schizophrenic mother (Schreiber, 1973). DID is also apparently relatively common, with rates of approximately 5% among psychiatric inpatients and 1% in the general population (Reinders & Veltman, 2021; Şar, Dorahy & Krüger, 2017). Despite this, Pica (1999) writes that "[p]erhaps no other disorder has endured as much scepticism as DID" (p. 405), and the legitimacy of DID as a genuine disorder remains an ongoing source of controversy (Kihlstrom, 2005; Lyn et al., 2014; Piper & Mersky, 2004a, 2004b).

The trauma-dissociation link is generally traced back to Pierre Janet's study of hysteria and hypnosis in France during the turn of the 20th century (Dell, 2009; Van der Hart & Horst, 1989; Van der Hart & Dorahy, 2023, 2014). Janet's work

DOI: 10.4324/9781003328254-1

was relatively forgotten until a "renaissance" of interest on the subject first arose during the 1970s and then especially in the 1980s–1990s (Cardeña, 1994; Diseth, 2005; Van der Hart & Dorahy, 2014). Janet's work is now widely regarded as providing the basis for contemporary theories of dissociation (see Van der Hart & Horst, 1989; Van der Hart & Dorahy, 2023; Van der Kolk, Herron & Hostetler, 1994), and advocates of the trauma-dissociation link believe that the vast majority of evidence supports the view that traumatisation causes pathological dissociation and DID (Bailey & Brand, 2017; Dalenberg et al., 2012, 2014; Dorahy et al., 2014; Raison & Andrea, 2023; Reinders & Veltman, 2021; Şar, Dorahy & Krüger, 2017). Dorahy et al. (2014) go so far as to write that "[e]very study that has systematically examined aetiology has found that antecedent severe, chronic childhood trauma is present in the histories of almost all individuals with DID" (p. 408, italics in original). Given this relationship, DID has been further taken to reflect a severe form of posttraumatic stress disorder (PTSD) (Reinders & Veltman, 2021; Şar, Dorahy & Krüger, 2017).

In contradistinction to the trauma-dissociation view is a position variously described as the socio-cognitive, fantasy, or iatrogenic view.[1] This position proposes that trauma plays no special role in the dissociative disorders and that DID is really a disorder of self-understanding influenced by social factors, expectations, and individual differences such as suggestibility (Lilienfeld, 1999; Lynn et al., 2014; Lynn et al., 2019; Spanos, 1994). Lynn et al. (2014), for example, write that DID occurs

> when people with coexisting or ambiguous psychological symptoms are exposed to suggestive procedures (e.g., repeated questioning about memories & personality "parts," leading questions, hypnosis, … media influences (e.g., film & television), and broader sociocultural expectations (e.g., "dissociation is associated with abuse," people possess "multiple personalities") regarding the presumed clinical features of DID.
>
> (p. 897)

Although traumatic experiences may nevertheless play a non-specific role (along with aversive experiences such as loneliness or sleep deprivation), any reported trauma might also reflect a mistaken memory or fantasy arising out of iatrogenic factors or other sources. Regarding the aforementioned case of Sybil, for instance, critics argue that the proposed explanation linking trauma to dissociation has been "thoroughly discredited", proposing instead that iatrogenic factors offer a more plausible account (Kihlstrom, 2005, p 243; cf. Paris, 2012, 2019).

Several findings do lend credence to the socio-cognitive account, as seen in the documented shifts in DID over time, including an apparent rise in the reported number of potential identities (Kihlstrom, 2005; Piper & Merskey, 2004a). For instance, 18th- and 19th-century cases typically reported dual personalities, described in terms such as "doubling of the ego", "double personality", or "alternating personality" (Janet, 1901; see also Van der Hart & Dorahy, 2023).[2] Morton Prince later reported the case of Miss Beauchamp with four personalities (Prince, 1906), and Janet (1907a) commented on cases with "as many as nine or ten" dissociative parts (p. 83). DSM-III (1980), however, accommodated up to 100 different personalities, while Kluft (2006) refers to cases of thousands. This proliferation has allowed critics to declare that such personality complexity is simply implausible:

> Despite the almost-infinite number of possible synaptic connections in the brain, one might say that the mind simply is not big enough to hold so many personalities. The proliferation of alter egos within cases, as well as the proliferation of cases, has been one of the factors leading to skepticism about the disorder itself.
> (Kihlstrom, 2005, p. 231)

The nature of the dissociative parts has also witnessed changes. For example, the 19th century dissociative parts were reportedly all human, whereas later 20th century cases report ones that are of different sex and race to the host, and even different species (e.g., Hendrickson, McCarty, & Goodwin, 1990). Such changes have prompted critics to ask, "[w]hy did the perhaps half-plausible 19th-century concept so floridly metamorphose into the totally implausible 20th-century concept?" (Piper & Merskey, 2004a, p. 597). Shifts in DID phenomenology have also been reported, including changes of executive control (the transitions from one personality state to another or "switching"). Switching reported in 19th century cases was typically subtle or sometimes occurred during sleep. For example, in Janet's (1907a) depiction of the case of "Lady of MacNish", switching involved being "suddenly seized, without previous warning, with a profound sleep, which lasted several hours longer than usual" (p. 68). With modern DID, however, switching can occur much more rapidly ("the time required to switch from one identity to another is usually a matter of seconds"—APA, 1994, p. 485). Based on such evidence, critics conclude that we should abandon "the simplistic, outdated trauma-dissociation model that Janet... proposed more than a century ago" (Lynn et al., 2014, p. 906).

Should we reject the possibility of trauma-dissociation and DID?

Despite such criticisms, other writers claim that, if anything, the scientific evidence for trauma-dissociation and DID is actually increasing (Brand et al., 2016; Martínez-Taboas et al., 2013). For example, Raison and Andrea's (2023) recent systematic review concluded that "it would seem the trauma theory has more evidence to support it than the iatrogenic theory" (p. 10), and emerging neurobiological evidence appears to also provide preliminary support favouring the trauma-dissociation position (Blihar et al., 2020; Reinders & Veltman, 2021). For example, smaller hippocampal volumes are found with both PTSD and DID (Chalavi et al., 2015), which is taken to be consistent with the view that DID is a severe form of PTSD (Reinders & Veltman, 2021; Şar, Dorahy & Krüger, 2017).

Nevertheless, assessing the veracity of trauma-dissociation and DID is complicated for several reasons. On the one hand, it is not simply a matter of comparing the theories with the evidence, partly because the existing evidence is interpreted in contradictory ways. Boysen (2011), for instance, notes that the evidence for either the socio-cognitive or trauma-dissociation models is "difficult to confirm or refute because the models offer contradictory interpretations of the same evidence" (p. 332). Both advocates and critics further recognise that it is extremely difficult to convincingly demonstrate that trauma causes dissociative pathology. Aside from the obvious ethical and practical issues with studying trauma in the laboratory (Lilienfeld et al., 1999; Van der Kolk & Fisler, 1995), any link between traumatisation and psychopathology is generally derived from both cross-sectional evidence and retrospective reports. As such, studies purporting to establish the trauma-dissociation link are typically incapable of ruling out alternative, and often more parsimonious explanations (Kihlstrom, 2005; McNally, 2003a, 2003b). For instance, any evidence for dissociative amnesia is commonly re-interpreted in terms of ordinary forgetting, infantile amnesia, or hesitancy in reporting the abuse (Kihlstrom, 2005; Manguilli et al., 2022; Paris, 2012).[3]

What complicates matters further is that both sets of theories might have valid application. Proponents of trauma-dissociation, for instance, recognise that it is entirely possible that some individuals, either deliberately or unknowingly, adopt DID characteristics based on socio-cultural influences (Dorahy et al., 2014). At the same time, the finding that some cases of DID may be iatrogenic by-products does not invalidate actual cases of trauma-induced DID, as Kihlstrom (2005) recognises:

> … the fact that dissociative symptomatology is embedded in the patient's social context does not necessarily invalidate the diagnostic category itself. Even schizophrenia has a sociocultural overlay. Nor does the possibility that some— probably many, perhaps most—recent cases of DID and other dissociative disorders are iatrogenic or misdiagnosed mean that the occasional genuine case should not be taken seriously. As rare as they may be, the dissociative disorders provide a unique perspective on fundamental questions concerning consciousness, identity, the self, and the unity of personality. As complex as they surely are, they deserve to be studied in a spirit of open inquiry that avoids both the excessive credulity of the enthusiast and the dismissal of the determined skeptic.
>
> (p. 244)

Moreover, the socio-cognitive and trauma-dissociation models are not necessarily wholly contradictory with one another since there is no logical objection to social and cultural factors shaping the expression of dissociative disorders (Dorahy et al., 2014; Şar et al., 2017). This possibility is especially apparent with the addition of "possession states" as potential diagnostic criteria for DID in DSM-5 (2013), where DID was broadened to encompass "the disruption of identity characterized by two or more distinct personality states *or an experience of possession*" (p. 292, italics added). Possession states themselves occur when "an individual experiences being taken over or inhabited by an external force, which then controls or changes that individual's actions and identity" (Bhavsar, Ventriglio & Bhugra, 2016, p. 553). Possession experiences are reported throughout human history and across diverse cultural settings (including within Western contexts; Hilgard, 1977; Spanos, 1994).[4] Of course, not all possession states are necessarily a sign of DID (Bhavsar et al., 2016; Dorahy et al., 2014), but the inclusion of possession states in DID criteria acknowledges the possibility that manifestations of DID may be influenced by an individual's cultural background (APA, 2022). Thus, in contexts where possession states have greater cultural familiarity than the concept of "personality","the identity alteration is attributed to possession by an external spirit, power, deity, or other person" (Spiegel et al., 2013, p. 303). Igreja et al.'s (2010) study of 941 adults in post-civil war Mozambique, for example, reports that at least 18.6% of sample were possessed by one spirit and that a further 5.6% were possessed by two or more spirits, possibly indicating a culturally congruent form of DID in response to traumatisation from the civil war. Whether this is actually the case or not is an empirical question, but at least one point of agreement between trauma-dissociation and socio-cognitive theorists concerns the role that sociocultural factors play in shaping personality and its disorders (cf. Lilienfeld, 1999).

Making sense of dissociation

Evidence aside, a major stumbling block to making sense of trauma-dissociation and assessing the legitimacy of DID is the very concept of dissociation itself. As Cardeña and Gleaves (2007) write, "there is no consensus on what dissociation actually means" (p. 474). Dissociation is sometimes described as a psychological process, a psychological structure, a psychological defence, a deficit, or a symptom (Cardeña & Gleaves, 2007). As a result, Dorahy and Van der Hart (2007) note that, "[d]epending on how it is understood, the construct of dissociation describes many psychological phenomena or few" (p. 6; cf. Dell, 2009). Any attempt then to accommodate these various meanings into a singular conceptualisation would make the concept too broad to be practical. Cardeña (1994), for instance, writes:

> Were we to accept every instance of unawareness, purposeful automatic behavior, or divided attention as an example of dissociation, we would have to conclude that we live our lives in perpetual dissociation, as there are always some stimuli that have a demonstrable effect on us or behaviors that we are not reflectively aware of, but which we nonetheless enact. ... In sum, the use of the term dissociation as shorthand for any kind of nonconscious or alternate mental process is of questionable merit.
>
> (p. 18)

Van der Hart and Dorahy (2014) thus rightly observe that the crux of the problem here is conceptual, writing, "there continues to a very large conceptual problem: Namely, there is little agreement about (1) the definition or meaning of dissociation, and (2) the specific psychological phenomena to which the construct refers" (p. 4). Nijenhuis (2015) further writes that going forward here requires immediate attention to this conceptual issue:

> What is … urgent is the formulation of consistent and viable concepts of dissociation, dissociative symptoms, and dissociative disorders to replace the current confusion in the DSM-5 and literature more generally… The core problem thus is the current confusing, inconsistent, partly over-inclusive and partly under-inclusive conceptualization of dissociation and dissociative disorders.
>
> (p. 76)

Conceptual problems are not, of course, uncommon in psychological science. One need only consider, for example, the long-standing contention concerning how best to conceptualise "psychological disorder" (see Zachar, 2000; Zachar & Krueger, 2013). Janet (1907a), himself, observes that the dissociative disorders present themselves in multifarious forms rather than occurring as discrete natural "kinds" or types. Be this as it may, conceptual and theoretical clarity is needed prior to examining the evidence for trauma-dissociation and DID. As Petocz and Newbery (2010) write, conceptual analysis plays a primary role in scientific enquiry in two senses:

> If the logical tests are failed, if our conceptual analysis reveals confusions, ambiguities, contradictions, implicit assumptions, and so forth, then we know without going any further (i.e., without taking the next step into any specific observational analysis) that the situation as envisaged is either *not yet clear enough* or *could not possibly be the case*. We are then constrained, in accordance with the requirements of scientific investigation, to reconsider the question, reformulate it, clarify it, adjust it, or abandon it. This reveals the *second* sense in which conceptual analysis is primary; it has the power to *preclude* observational inquiry, whereas observational analysis can never reveal that conceptual analysis is inappropriate.
>
> (p. 130, italics in original)

Thus, conceptual and theoretical analysis is necessary for helping to resolve the controversy concerning trauma-dissociation and DID.

On description and explanation

The lack of definitional consensus spills over into other important conceptual issues. One such conceptual issue concerns the dual explanatory and descriptive roles attributed to dissociation. Dissociation is sometimes described as a *cause* of symptoms (e.g., a defensive process leading to symptomatology) and at other times the dissociative symptoms themselves (Cardeña & Gleaves, 2007). Moreover, these two usages are often conflated. Dell (2009), for instance, writes that "almost all portrayals of dissociation are quite vague about what causes it" (p. 722) but at the same time observes that dissociation is also largely used implicitly in an explanatory sense (i.e., dissociation acts as the *cause* of those same symptoms). Additionally, both critics and advocates alike acknowledge that any singular sense of "dissociation" will be too broad to explain the diverse array of dissociative phenomena (Brown, 2006; Cardeña, 1994; Jureidini, 2004), with some then blurring the distinction between cause and phenomenon-to-be-explained. McNally (2003a), for example, writes:

> Part of the problem is that diverse phenomena are subsumed under the vague and global rubric of dissociation. Consider the psychological phenomena often characterized as dissociative: derealization, flashbacks, depersonalization, out-of-body experiences, a sense of time slowing down (or speeding up), emotional numbing, and an inability to remember otherwise presumably memorable aspects of the traumatic event (amnesia). ... Defined in this abstract, global way, dissociation cannot possibly count as a "mechanism" for anything. The term undoubtedly embraces diverse psychobiological processes. For example, it seems inconceivable that the subjective experience of time slowing down can possibly be related to the mechanisms of an out-of-body experience. Progress in understanding acute response to trauma will come by splitting the global concept of dissociation into its constituents, not by lumping diverse phenomena under the same label.
>
> (p. 785)

McNally's comment here draws attention to the critical importance of clearly addressing the distinction between causal mechanisms and phenomenon to be explained. Instances such as flashbacks and out-of-body experiences could be viewed as the phenomena requiring explanation, and yet McNally's apparent expectation here is that these phenomena might also count as mechanisms.

Conceptual problems further extend to the concept of "trauma". Weathers and Keane (2008) here write that although "[t]rauma is a fundamental concept in the field of traumatic stress, ... it is difficult to define and has been the source of much controversy" (p. 657). In a similar fashion to dissociation, the concept of trauma is understood variously (Sandler et al., 1991), and at times treated as both the cause of psychopathology and as the effect of extremely stressful events. Zepf and Zepf (2008), for example, note that

> there is often no distinction made ... as to whether trauma is thought of as the event itself or the experience of it. At times trauma is regarded as the process of traumatization, the traumatic state, and at other times it refers to the permanent subsidiary changes in the affected subject.
>
> (p. 331)

Muddying the waters further is the recognition that the terms "dissociation" and "trauma" might actually function as metaphors (Nijenhuis, 2019). There is, of course, nothing wrong with metaphors *per se*, and all scientific fields employ metaphors and analogy for illustrative purposes (Cheshire & Thomä, 1991). However, the scientific value of any metaphor requires "marking off the area of negative analogy". This entails understanding the relevant characteristics of both the phenomenon and metaphor, as well as knowing the essential points of difference (Cheshire & Thomä, 1991). If we do not have a clear understanding of what the terms trauma and dissociation refer to, then it is not possible to distinguish between what these terms actually refer to and what they might actually only resemble.

The structural theory of dissociation

One recent attempt to address the confusion surrounding the concept of dissociation is the theory of trauma-related structural dissociation, hereafter referred to simply as the structural theory[5] (Dorahy & Van der Hart, 2007; Nijenhuis et al., 2010; Steele et al., 2014b; Van der Hart et al., 2004, 2006, 2023). Van der Hart and Dorahy (2023) distinguish between broad and narrow perspectives on dissociation, with the former centred on phenomena such as altered states of consciousness (including depersonalisation and derealisation), and the latter pertaining to structural aspects or personality organisation. While contemporary attention largely focuses upon dissociative phenomena mapped along a spectrum of dissociative functioning, advocates of the structural theory contend that this approach does not adequately address dissociative phenomena (Van der Hart et al., 2004; Van der Hart & Dorahy, 2023)). To address this, these authors advocate restricting the concept of dissociation to align with Janet's structural division of the personality. On this view, the term "dissociative" applies "only to the phenomena produced by the divided mind or divided personalities, and therefore dissociative phenomena have a single origin (i.e., division in the personality/multiplication of personalities)" (Van der Hart & Dorahy, 2023, p. 30). This leads to criteria for judging whether any phenomenon reflects dissociation or not: "...*a symptom can be said to be dissociative only if (1) there is clear evidence of dissociative parts of the personality, and (2) the symptom is found in one or some parts of the personality but not others*" (Steele et al., 2014b, p. 249, their italics). Accordingly, symptoms typically considered prototypically dissociative (e.g., derealisation, absorption) may not actually be dissociative, whereas other symptoms generally not considered dissociative (e.g., suicidality, substance abuse, self-harm), may, in fact, be, if the conditions of structural dissociation are met (Steele et al., 2014b; Van der Hart et al., 2006). Following Janet, Van der Hart and Dorahy (2023) go on to propose at least two variants of dissociative phenomena: hypnotically induced divisions (e.g., artificial somnambulism) and trauma-induced divisions, where dissociated parts are either trauma-avoidant or trauma-fixated.

The structural theory extends upon Janet's work by further integrating the work of Charles Samuel Myers (1940). Myers observed that acutely traumatised World War I combat soldiers would come to experience co-existing or alternating states of both avoidance of, and fixation upon, the traumatising event(s). This presentation provides the foundation for the core symptoms and diagnosis of PTSD today (e.g., DSM-5; APA, 2022), and is taken to represent a *sine qua non* of trauma-related disorders (Steele et al., 2014b; Van der Hart et al., 2006). These contradictory responses are taken to reflect actual divisions of "personality" arising as a result of traumatisation. These dissociative parts are described as the "Apparently Normal part (or parts) of the Personality" (ANP) and the "Emotional Part (or parts) of the Personality (EP) (Nijenhuis et al., 2010; Steele et al. 2014b; Van der Hart et al., 2006). The former is typically associated with managing daily life, whereas the latter reflects defensive responses to the traumatising circumstances. These dissociative parts are themselves based upon evolutionary-shaped action systems (Nijenhuis et al., 2010; Steele et al., 2014b; Van der Hart et al., 2006), and so trauma-related dissociation "refers to the existence of at least two self-organising *systems of psychobiological states*" (Steele et al., 2014b, p. 239, italics in original).

As well as addressing the discrepant findings within the literature, the structural theory's aim here is also explanatory since the theorists "sought a theory that could explain *all* dissociative symptoms" (Steele et al., 2014b, p. 240, italics in original). In line with Janet's theory, traumatisation here plays a key explanatory role since "components of the personality or consciousness ... become divided from each other under conditions of extreme stress" (Steele et al., 2014b, p. 239). The theory here also has far reaching implications since these dissociative parts are not restricted to DID but are also found in trauma-related disorders such as PTSD. In this context, the structural theory acknowledges that the severity of trauma can result in the emergence of numerous dissociative parts, manifesting in varying degrees of division—primary, secondary, and tertiary structural dissociation (Steele et al., 2014b; Van der Hart et al., 2006).[6] With simple PTSD, for instance, an ANP and EP become structurally dissociated from one another (*primary structural dissociation*), whereas both a single ANP and multiple EPs arise in cases of Complex PTSD (*secondary structural dissociation*). On the other hand, with *tertiary structural dissociation*—characteristic of DID—there are both multiple ANPs and EPs (Nijenhuis et al., 2010; Steele et al., 2014b; Van der Hart et al., 2006). Consequently, something resembling multiple personalities occurs across a range of phenomena outside of DID.

Dissociation and the puzzle of personality

Naturally, not everyone agrees with the structural theory's attempt to limit the definition of dissociation. Critics have accused the structural theory of adopting an overly restrictive and dogmatic approach, particularly considering the diverse ways that the term "dissociation" is currently used (e.g., Bowman, 2011; Brown, 2011; Dell, 2009, 2011; Ross, 2014). Dell (2011), for instance, believes that basing all trauma-derived disorders such as PTSD on structural dissociation conflicts with the available empirical evidence. Several authors further challenge the re-categorisation of prototypical "dissociative phenomena" like derealisation and absorption as non-dissociative alterations of consciousness if not based on structural dissociation (Brown, 2011; Dell, 2011).

At the same time, various authors also recognise that definitional disputes can easily go around in circles (see Frewen, Brand & Lanius, 2022; Ross, 2014). Rather than then attempting to address how best to define dissociation, the interest in the present work is to critically examine the theoretical claims made concerning trauma-dissociation and the nature of consciousness and personality in accounts of DID. Personality here needs to be appreciated within its appropriate context, however. The first modern accounts of DID emerged when "personality" pertained primarily to the conscious self as a knowing agent, rather than the more current focus upon traits associated with personality research today (cf. Zachar & Krueger, 2013). Within this original context, then, DID, on the face of it, appears to entail multiple persons or "streams of consciousness", each with its own first-person perspective and experience of a separate sense of selfhood (Nijenhuis, 2012, 2015; Nijenhuis et al., 2010; Özturk & Şar, 2016; Van der Hart et al., 2006). Şar, Dorahy, & Krüger (2017), for instance, write that "each of these identities reports their own subjective experiences and memories, their own sense of agency and will, and their own perspective on who they are" (p. 138). Manning and Manning (2007) similarly describe DID as "a condition in which more than one person appears to inhabit a single body" (p. 841). Consequently, DID raises the "possibility that two or more streams of consciousness or identity states coexist in one body" (Cardeña & Gleaves, 2007, p. 487), which strongly challenges our common-sense view of persons.

Whether the dissociative parts found in DID should be taken to be literally distinct persons or personalities is unclear, however. In relation to this, Merckelbach et al. (2002) pose the question as to whether dissociative parts should "be considered as metaphors for differing emotional states or as genuine entities that have their own memory or identity, which are truly autonomous, and are therefore capable of willful action" (p. 482). In the former sense, dissociative parts are ordinary experiences of a single agent mis-characterised as separate identities, whereas with the latter, the parts are agents, each with their own motives and experiences. The socio-cognitive perspective discussed earlier supports the former: DID is considered a disorder of self-understanding, whereby multiple role enactments provide the basis for the mistaken view of multiple personalities, primarily influenced by iatrogenic and socio-cultural factors (Lilienfeld et al., 1999; Lynn et al., 2014, 2019; Spanos, 1994). Lilienfeld et al. (1999), for instance, write that "DID patients adopt and enact social roles geared to their aspirations and the demand characteristics of varied social contexts...the role and 'self' (or 'multiple selves' as the case may be) coalesce so as to become essentially indistinguishable" (p. 508). Consequently, there is really only a single self rather than independent multiple personalities, and on this point, Lynn et al. (2014) explicitly state: "When we use the term *dissociation*, we typically refer to dissociative experiences or symptoms, not to a literal splitting of different aspects of consciousness or multiple personalities" (p. 897*n*, italics in original).

It is with respect to this view above where we find agreement between proponents of the socio-cognitive perspective and proponents of trauma-dissociation. Some proponents of trauma-dissociation similarly argue against the notion that any individual literally has multiple personalities, suggesting instead that a single individual erroneously perceives themselves as composed of distinct entities (or possessed by outside agencies). Dalenberg et al. (2012) thus note their agreement here with the socio-cognitive position: "We do not disagree that DID is in part a disorder of self-understanding. Clearly those with DID have the inaccurate idea that they are more than one person" (p. 568; cf. Spiegel et al., 2013). Dalenberg et al. (2012) further state that they:

> … do not take at face value DID identities' prevalent beliefs that they actually are "real people" with varying demographic and psychological characteristics, including differing ages, genders, etc. Nor would proponents of either model take at face value other common beliefs that alternate identities are animals, mythical beings, internalized "outside" people, demons, or omniscient beings.
>
> (p. 568)

In relation to clinical work, then, Spiegel (2006) writes that "[a] clinician can note that a patient experiences him/herself as having more than one identity or personality state without believing that there really are four people in that body" (p. 577). The shifting terminology associated with DID also reflects a move away from viewing the disorder in terms of distinct personalities. Spiegel (2006) here explains that the shift away from Multiple Personality Disorder (APA, 1980) was in fact to re-correct the emphasis away from multiple "persons":

> … changing the name of multiple personality disorder to dissociative identity disorder [was] to place the correct emphasis on the failure to integrate aspects of identity, memory, and consciousness rather than the apparent proliferation of "personalities." Indeed, the problem is not having more than one personality, it is having less than one. The components of such a personality structure are often quite limited, associated with one primary affect or segment of experiences. This fragmentation complicates the patient's ability to respond to complex life circumstances and form meaningful relationships. The other change involved one word: "presence" instead of "existence" of more than one identity or personality state. The term "presence" was drawn from the description of delusions in schizophrenia. One can describe a patient's delusions without believing them.
>
> (p. 577)

As such, both critics and advocates view DID as a disorder of self-understanding, with the difference between these positions primarily concerning whether this is a genuine disorder with traumatisation at its core.

On personality and its disorders

A major problem throughout this discussion, however, is that the specific meaning of "personality" is rarely, if ever, addressed. Consequently, it is difficult to assess the specific claims being made. By way of example, Spanos (1994) believes that DID patients "come to believe that their alter identities are real personalities rather than self-generated fantasies" (p. 144), but fails to ever address what constitutes a "real personality". Merckelbach, Devilly, and Rassina (2002) similarly attempt to evaluate whether dissociative parts constitute genuine personalities, without first addressing the criteria for defining a "real" personality. A similar issue occurs with the term "self". For example, Lynn et al. (2019) recently write that "individuals with DID hold the mistaken belief that they house separate selves" (p. 3), but leave open the question as to what these "selves" might actually be.[7] The need for clarity here further extends to the nature of "consciousness", as seen in this example from Putnam (1992):

> The implicit and mistaken assumption made by many people is that the alter personalities are separate people. This is a serious conceptual error that will lead to therapeutic error. Alter personalities are not separate people! Rather, I think that they are best conceptualized as examples of a fundamental and discrete unit of consciousness, the behavioral state. Behavioral states are specific patterns of psychological and physiological variables that occur together and repeat themselves, often in highly predictable sequences, and that are relatively stable and enduring over time.
>
> (p. 96)

Putnam's position is also reflected in Dalenberg et al. (2020) who similarly write that rather than multiple persons, "we have repeatedly described these individuals as suffering from a fragmentation of identity with personified behavioral states" (p. 134). However, the relationship here between behavioural states and consciousness requires greater clarification. For example, Putnam (1992) also provides a room metaphor, whereby "[t]he alters exist together as a 'family' and differentiate themselves from yet another set of alters that dwell in the 'other room'" (p. 100). If these alters exist *simultaneously* and can differentiate themselves from one another, then this appears to mean that the dissociative parts are independent knowers, rather than simply behavioural acts under the domain of a single "consciousness" or self. Whatever the case may be, the dissociative parts appear to explicitly constitute independent knowers within the structural theory (Nijenhuis, 2012, 2015; Nijenhuis et al., 2010; Van der Hart et al., 2006): "The cardinal feature of patients with dissociative disorders is that they involve multiple first-person perspectives" (Nijenhuis, 2012, p. 143).

What the above illustrates is that without clear conceptualisation and theory of personality processes and dissociative phenomena, it is impossible to precisely know what is being defended or attacked in debates concerning DID and the dissociative disorders. Furthermore, given that the problem with making sense of trauma-dissociation and DID is conceptual in nature, any solution must also be conceptually oriented. Van der Hart and Dorahy (2023) thus aptly observe that

> [c]larity may be assisted by clearly differentiating and defining the following terms and how they relate to one another: dissociation, personality,

consciousness, identity, state (i.e., mental state, state of consciousness, ego state, identity state, self-state), alter personality, dissociative personality and dissociative parts of the personality.

(p. 31)

Consequently, making sense of dissociative parts requires a thoroughgoing account of so-called normal personality and the nature of self and consciousness.

Such conceptual concerns are not simply of theoretical interest or idle philosophy since resolving these issues has clinical implications (Merckelbach et al., 2002; Paris, 2019; Putnam, 1992). By way of example, the controversy surrounding the specific nature of DID impacts upon diagnosis and misdiagnosis (Brand et al., 2016; Reinders & Veltman, 2021). Kihlstrom (2005), here, observes, that "difficulties defining such terms as "personality", "identity", and "ego state"—not to mention "amnesia" itself—can inject an unacceptable level of subjectivity into the diagnosis" (p. 229; cf. Paris, 2012). Critics, then, are quick to note that ostensibly similar phenomena such as bipolar disorder, borderline personality disorder, and even schizophrenia can be confused with DID (Kihlstrom, 2005; Paris, 2012; Piper & Mersky, 2004a). Janet (1907a), for instance, reports the case of Felida X from France who alternated between states of melancholy and cheerfulness. This example could potentially be understood in terms of bipolar disorder rather than in terms of dissociated identities. Kihlstrom (2005) thus writes: "When enthusiastic clinicians are determined to find it, DID can be diagnosed merely from the normal situational variability of behavior, or instances where otherwise 'normal' people just 'don't feel like themselves'" (p. 229). However, such a statement assumes that we understand what a "normal" person is, and because we simply do not have such an understanding, it is not possible to evaluate how best to interpret such cases.

The aim of the present work

The aim of the present work is to address the clarity and coherency of accounts of trauma-dissociation and to make sense of the nature of personality and consciousness within theories of DID. As discussed earlier, both advocates and critics alike recognise that conceptual and theoretical confusion pervades the field of dissociation (Cardeña & Gleaves, 2007; Kihlstrom, 2005; Nijenhuis & Van der Hart, 2011; Van der Hart et al., 2004). The aim here, however, is not to attempt to prove any one theory correct, but rather to assess what stands up to logical scrutiny with respect to causal claims about trauma and dissociation, along with the meaning of personal identity, consciousness, and personhood when discussing the dissociative disorders. To achieve this requires addressing the conceptual and theoretical understanding of trauma and dissociative responses, along with what constitutes "the person". Clarifying this requires first setting up a conceptual framework suitable for assessing the relation between trauma and dissociation and the nature of self and personality. This framework extends to clarifying the concepts of both causality and explanation for understanding the impact of traumatisation, along with clarifying the nature of mind. The philosophical stance to be adopted here can be described as a realist one, and one that is consistent with a natural science framework. This position acknowledges the significance of the logic of "relations" for understanding the relationship between trauma and dissociation, mind and brain, self and identity, and conscious and unconscious mental processes (Boag, 2012, 2017).

There are, however, a number of barriers that need to be addressed when attempting to make sense of DID and the dissociative disorders. One of these involves our assumptions concerning the nature of personality and consciousness. As various authors recognise, the dissociative disorders challenge our whole sense of what it means to be a person, including assumptions held about the concept of self (Dorahy et al., 2014). Spiegel (2010) here writes:

> They [the dissociative disorders] are right at the border of could and would, losses of control over cognitive functions such as memory, identity, and consciousness, that we take pride in managing. They both result in severe mental dysfunction and yet seem transient (at least in overt presentation) and controllable. They force us to re-examine our assumptions about the solidity of identity and the consistency of our control over our minds and bodies.
>
> (p. 262)

The inclusion of possession states in DSM-5 (APA, 2013), while welcome, also complicates matters further by raising the question concerning how to best incorporate cultural dimensions into our theories of personality and dissociation. Concepts of personhood and identity, normal or otherwise, vary across cultures (Cardeña & Gleaves, 2007; Kirmayer, Adeponle & Dzokoto, 2018), and given that "[t]he main contrast between these two forms of DID appears to be shaped by the person's sociocultural milieu" (Spiegel et al., 2013, p. 304),[8] culture is inextricably bound to conceptions of both self and personality and thus DID. The situation is further complicated by the sheer number of causal factors contributing to DID. As Dorahy et al. (2014) write, "existing data demonstrate that development of DID is probably due to a complex combination of traumatic experiences, dissociative processes, psychosocial mediators and socially constructed understandings of self" (p. 408; cf. Şar et al., 2017). Thus, part of the challenge here involves addressing what it means to be a person with respect to mind, body, and culture. Here Seligman and Kirmayer (2008) write, "every complex human experience emerges from an interaction of individual biology and psychology with social context" (p. 24), and, as such, any adequate account of trauma-dissociation and DID needs to be able to embrace such factors.

In terms of achieving the aim of the present work, special attention will also be paid to the contributions made by the structural theory of dissociation (Van der Hart et al., 2006). The structural theory is the most comprehensive and clearly articulated account of trauma-dissociation and DID, and a critical analysis of the structural theory provides a basis for comparing the two major approaches for understanding trauma-dissociation: Janetian-type and Freudian-based, psychodynamic explanations. As developed earlier, the structural theory, based on Janet's (1901, 1907a) theory, proposes that trauma-related dissociation represents an "ongoing integrative *deficit* that results in a *structural dissociation* of the personality" (Steele et al., 2014b, p. 240, italics in original). This Janetian position stands in contrast to a Freudian-based psychodynamic approach postulating psychological defence against overwhelming affects (e.g., Diseth, 2005; Schimmenti, 2018).

One argument that will be put forward is that despite the important contributions made by the structural theory, the contention here is that the Janetian explanatory foundations of the theory are nevertheless untenable. As will be demonstrated, there are major conceptual problems with deficit accounts of trauma-dissociation and DID. Consequently, a different theoretical explanation is required to account for structural dissociation. However, as will also be developed, much psychodynamic theorising of dissociative defence is, itself, also problematic. The specific problem here is that dissociation is said to occur in order to protect the mind from trauma This, on the face of it, is teleological and so rules out the possibility of coherently explaining dissociative defence. Instead, if defence plays any role in dissociation, it will need to be a causally efficient one, and as will be advanced, a coherent psychodynamic foundation emerges within the structural theory itself. This foundation postulates that mammalian motivational systems provide the basis for understanding personality, normal or otherwise, a position which has far-reaching implications for understanding not only trauma-related pathology but also personality generally.

Notes

1 Hereafter referred to as the socio-cognitive view, to emphasise the importance of social and cultural factors, but acknowledging other influences such as fantasy proneness, sleep deprivation, and iatrogenesis.
2 Cases of DID can, of course, also be found before the rise of modern psychiatry and psychology, including within Biblical accounts (Stephenson, 2015).
3 Critics often also highlight the greater probability of remembering a traumatic event rather than forgetting it (e.g., hypermnesia) (Kihlstrom, 2005; Paris, 2012).
4 Following Spiegel et al. (2013), terms such as Western and non-Western cultural orientations are very broad brushstrokes that necessarily obscure the actual diversity of people living in different parts of the world (cf. Bandura, 2002). Such terms are used here simply as shorthand to describe broad cultural trends. Part of the problem for personality research is that most research is conducted with so-called WEIRD populations (Western, educated, industrialised, rich, and democratic societies—Jones, 2010), making it relatively easy to ignore how widespread the phenomenon of possession actually is. For a discussion of problems associated with objectively assessing cultural phenomena relevant to dissociation, see Bhavsar et al. (2016).
5 The use of the term "structural theory" here is not to be confused with the structural theory of the id, ego, and superego from Freudian theory (e.g., Freud, 1923b).
6 These degrees were initially described as "levels" (e.g., Van der Hart et al., 2006). However, Van der Hart (2021) recently proposes that the term "degrees" is more appropriate, to help avoid conceptual confusion with other models describing levels of dissociation.

7 Later, in this same paper, these authors discuss "self-representations", but such representations seem to be distinct from "selves" since these authors also write, "[i]n the case of DID, insofar as individuals do not actually possess separate selves, their disorder can be construed as an impairment in self-perception and self-awareness…" (Lynn et al., 2019, p. 4).
8 The distinction between east and west should not be overstated, however, since so-called culture-bound possession states are also found in Western contexts (Ross, Schroeder & Ness, 2014).

Chapter 2

Dissociation and the logic of relations

The preceding chapter established that both advocates and critics recognise that a core problem with making sense of trauma-dissociation and DID is conceptual (Cardeña & Gleaves, 2007; Kihlstrom, 2005; Nijenhuis, 2015; Van der Hart & Dorahy, 2023). One first step then for addressing this is to develop an approach for clarifying the relation between trauma and dissociation and the nature of dissociative personality parts. This further requires addressing the concepts of causality and explanation for understanding how trauma might impact upon individuals, as well as clarifying the nature of mind and personality. One way to go forward here is to employ conceptual analysis, which involves assessing the logical coherency of concepts, theories, and hypotheses (Petocz & Newbery, 2010). Conceptual research has a long history in science generally (Machado & Silva, 2007) and precedes empirical testing since theories must be clarified *prior* to empirical assessment. As Petocz and Newbery (2010) earlier point out,

> [i]f the logical tests are failed, if our conceptual analysis reveals confusions, ambiguities, contradictions, implicit assumptions, and so forth, then we know without going any further (i.e., without taking the next step into any specific observational analysis) that the situation as envisaged is either *not yet clear enough* or *could not possibly be the case*.
>
> (p. 130, italics in original)

Mackay (2006), thus, emphasises that "in the evaluation of any substantive theory and its evidence, priority must go to the logical test of the theory's propositions" (p. 40), simply because attempting to empirically assess theories that lack logical coherence would be futile since they cannot accurately correspond to reality.

There are, however, numerous potential avenues for conceptual research (see Banicki, 2012), and one immediate consideration here concerns underlying assumptions. Any approach inherently involves foundational "metaphysical" assumptions, whether explicitly acknowledged or not (Henriques, 2019; Hibberd, 2014; Nijenhuis, 2015). Metaphysics here simply refers to claims and suppositions concerning the nature of reality, which, in turn, inform what we take to be the nature of consciousness, personhood, and causality.[1] Addressing such suppositions is not

DOI: 10.4324/9781003328254-2

simply "philosophical" musing, since how we conceptualise such notions directly impacts upon clinical considerations, including mind-body relations (Nijenhuis, 2015). As will be developed below, the conceptual approach adopted here for making sense of dissociation and DID is consistent with a realist, natural science framework. This approach proposes a mind-independent reality that we can come to know directly.[2] Although there is some resistance to the proposal that there is a reality that we can objectively know (e.g., Nijenhuis, 2015), such realism provides a basis for an empirical, scientific psychology attempting to establish factual theories.[3]

The aim of this chapter is to establish a theoretical framework to serve as a basis for judging the coherency of theories of trauma-dissociation and DID. The chapter first addresses the concept of relation, before then turning to the distinction between description and explanation and the logical errors of reification and circular explanation. A case is made for viewing psychological processes as certain relations, and that clarifying the subject and object terms of the dissociative relation is important for addressing the knower in accounts of DID. Problems with teleological explanations and the apparent teleology found in purposive accounts of dissociative defence are also addressed.

A realist metaphysic

Despite the absence of consensus, dissociation is nevertheless typically defined as a relation whereby something x is dissociated from y (cf. Braude, 2014).[4] One valuable position for addressing the logic of relations emerges from the contributions of Scottish-born John Anderson (1962). The value in Anderson's work is, in part, due to clarifying the important, but often poorly appreciated, ontological distinction between *qualities* (or non-relational properties), *entities* (or "things" with their non-relational properties) and *relations*.[5] As Mackie (in Anderson, 1962) writes, "a quality is an intrinsic feature of a thing, it belongs to the thing itself, whereas a relation holds between two or more things" (p. 266). Any entity (or thing) consists of various qualities that can be described as intrinsic features or non-relational properties. Human beings, for example, embody various non-relational attributes including both physical and biological characteristics. Relations, on the other hand, involve at least two or more distinct *terms*[6] standing in relation to one another. For example, the spatial relation of "sitting on" describes the relation between two terms (e.g., the cup *sitting on* the table). "Meaning", on the other hand, is a ternary relation between the signifier, signified, and a cognising subject (Petocz, 1999).

One implication of this view of relations is that the terms involved possess their own intrinsic properties and are logically independent from each other. As Maze (1983) writes:

> Anything that can stand .... in any relation at all, must have at least some intrinsic properties. If that were not the case ... then we could not understand what it was that was said to have those relationships. A relation can only hold between

two or more terms, and a part of what is involved in seeing those terms as related is being able to see them as distinct, that is, as each having its own intrinsic properties, so that we can say what the terms *are* that are related. This means that each term of the relation must be able in principle to be described without the need to include any reference to its relation to the other.

(p. 24, italics in original)[7]

So, in the situation where Lucia is taller than Anne-Marie, both Lucia and Anne-Marie must exist and have properties that are intrinsic to each. However, the relation of difference is *between* those properties of Lucia and Anne-Marie rather than existing as a property of either person. This can be more formally written as the relation aRb cannot be reduced to either a or b alone. The relation itself is not, however, some type of substantive third entity. As Michell (1988) writes, a relation "is not a kind of *stuff* that binds the terms. It is just how the terms are with respect to each other" (p. 234, italics in original).

There are diverse types of relations (e.g., spatial, causal, temporal, logical, familial, and legal) and appreciating the logic of relations provides a means of conducting conceptual analysis in two important ways (Boag, 2017). First, any concept or theoretical term can be assessed for whether it refers to a property or quality of something (including whether it refers to an entity that consists of its own intrinsic properties), or instead refers to specific relations between qualities or entities. Secondly, any concept or theoretical term can be assessed with respect to the distinction between what something *is* said to be, and what it is said to *do*. We can distinguish, for example, between what the brain is (i.e., the brain consists of nerves, including neurons and blood vessels) and what it does (e.g., the brain allows thinking to occur). The brain's activities, if anything, simply describe a particular relationship (where the brain performs x). One consequence of this position is that if a theorist is proposing that a certain entity or quality exists, then it should have intrinsic features that can be identified independently of any relation entered into. The latter would mean describing the property independently of any particular performance or activity (Maze, 1983). Consequently, the onus is on the theorist to stipulate—at least in principle—what intrinsic features constitute such qualities or entities, independent of any activity that they perform.

Confusing terms and their relations

Following from this, saying what something is should not be confused with what it does, and there are several conceptual errors associated with failing to grasp the distinction between qualities and relations. One of these is the problem of reification. Reification is commonly conceptualised in terms of confusing the "abstract" with the "concrete" but is taken here to more specifically refer to mistaking relations with entities or their properties (Bell, Staines & Michell, 2001; Passmore, 1935). Reification generally arises from failing to recognise the logical independence of terms and mistakenly taking relationships between things to be either properties (or qualities) of things, or taking these relations to be the entities themselves. To use the earlier example, to say that Lucia is taller than Anne-Marie is to note a relationship between these two people. As a relation, "being taller" cannot be reduced solely to a property of either Lucia or Anne-Marie. However, to misconceptualise "being taller" as an intrinsic feature of (in this case) Lucia would be to reify the relationship (i.e., to mistakenly treat tallness as a property). In this manner, reification can easily occur when mistaking differences between individuals with an individual's intrinsic features.

Closer to psychology, mistaking differences between individuals with an individual's intrinsic features is not uncommon in personality research. This is evident when differences identified in personality assessment *between* individuals are mistakenly confused with within-person attributes (see Boag, 2011, 2018; Borsboom, Mellenbergh & van Heerden, 2003; Cervone, 2004, 2005; Lamiell, 2007, 2013). For example, knowing that someone is "extraverted" tells us where someone sits upon the dimension of extraversion in relation to other people. This is comparative information, which tells us nothing about the within-subject attributes underlying such variation. However, this comparative information is, at times, mistakenly reified into within-subject attributes ("traits") that are then held to be causally responsible for that same trait behaviour (e.g., as proposed by the Five Factor Model and Theory (McCrae, 2004; McCrae & Costa, 1995, 2008; see Boag, 2011, 2015, 2018; Cervone, 2004, 2005 for further discussion).

A related error here concerns the fallacy of constitutive relations, which is to "treat relations as if they were terms, entities possessing independent natures of their own" (McMullen, 1996, p. 61). This fallacy involves constituting an entity or thing solely in terms of its relatedness to other things, rather than in terms of its intrinsic properties (Maze, 1983). An example of this is apparent in some accounts postulating a "self" acting as an agent (i.e., the 'doer' standing in the doing relation). On the logic of relations described above, if the self is a term engaging in cognition and performing activities, then any such self should have intrinsic features that are logically independent from that which it is said to do. However, we find accounts proposing that the self is somehow both an agent and a relation. For example, Macmurray (1961, 1969) proposes that the self is a cognising agent that performs various activities. Given the logic of relations discussed above, such a self should stand as the subject term in the doing and knowing relations (i.e., the agent S that does x or the agent S that knows p). However, Macmurray (1961) also claims that the self is constituted by relatedness: "[T]he Self exists only in dynamic relation with the Other [the world] ... the Self is constituted by its relation to the Other'" (p. 17). If it is the case that the "self" is constituted by relatedness, then this leaves unanswered what the "it" is that has those same relations (cf. Maze, 1983). Consequently, if, as Macmurray proposes, the self or knower exists solely in relation to other entities (i.e., lacking intrinsic qualities of its own), then it succumbs to the fallacy of constitutive relations. In other words, the "self as agent", as proposed by Macmurray, cannot stand as the subject having those same relations (see Boag, 2005 for further discussion).

Description and explanation

The discussion of reification above further bears upon the topics of causality and explanation. Causality is also a relation (between causes and effects) and, as such, these terms need to be logically independent of one another if we are to speak sensibly about something causing something else. One potential problem that can arise here involves confusing description with explanation. Broadly speaking, description involves classification (taxonomy), while explanation addresses the causal factors responsible for bringing the observed phenomena into being (Boag, 2011, 2018). Description is logically independent of explanation because it is possible to describe something without providing an explanation for it. For example, knowing that someone suffers from anxiety does not tell us about the specific processes that explain how those symptoms came into being (cf. Brown, 2011). However, although both description and explanation have their rightful place in science, confusing description with explanation is problematic because it leads to *circular explanation* (Boag, 2011). Circular explanation occurs when the explanation of some effect (the *explanans*) is equivalent to the effect that it is said to explain (the *explanandum*), such that the explanation for some occurrence is essentially the occurrence itself (Bell et al., 2001; Boag, 2011; 2017).

Circular explanation easily occurs when a *description* of behaviour is mistakenly used to explain that same behaviour. This has been described as "verbal-magic": "giving a name to a certain kind of event and then using the name as if it accounted for the *occurrence* of that kind of event" (Maze, 1954, p. 226; italics in original). For example, it might seem reasonable to explain someone's forgetting being due to amnesia. However, *if* amnesia simply means not being able to remember (e.g., Drever, 1952), then using amnesia to "explain" someone's memory failure is circular because the effect is not logically distinct from the cause.[8] Such verbal magic is apparent with respect to personality traits discussed above, as well as theories postulating "abilities" or "capacities". We read, for instance, that someone is able to perform well on mathematical tests because they possess high "mathematical ability", as if the ability is some type of property that causes that same performance (e.g., Nunes et al., 2012; cf. Howe, 1990). However, such abilities are typically defined in terms of what they are attempting to explain (i.e., the ability to do *X*). As such, the "ability", if anything, is simply what the person is *able to do*—a description of performance or likely performance—rather than the cause or explanation of that same ability.[9]

The problem of circular explanation has been raised at various times in the history of modern psychological science (Maze, 1954; Skinner, 1953),[10] and avoiding circular explanation involves appreciating Hume's (1911/1739) position that causes must precede effects, and that causes and effects must be logically distinct from one another (i.e., if *A* causes *B,* then *A* ≠ *B)*. This means that any satisfactory explanatory term "has characters of its own which can be examined quite apart from their effects on other things" (Passmore, 1935, p. 280; cf. Maze, 1983). To suggest otherwise would mean that the effect already exists and brings itself into being, thereby rendering cause-effect relationships to nonsense. As Mackay more formally notes,

> [c]ausation is a relation between two independent events. For event or process C to be a cause of an event E, the effect, C must exist independently of E, and E cannot happen before it. They must be events or processes separate in space and time.
>
> (Mackay, 1996, p. 10)

Consequently, in postulating that C causes E, C must be distinct from E. If E is a re-description of C, or C contains E (such that CE causes E) then C and E are not independent—and any such causal claim is tantamount to saying that E already exists to bring itself into existence (cf. Passmore, 1935).

Causality and causal explanation

The topic of causal explanation is, of course, complex (see Mackie, 1974) but on the position here, all events arise out of antecedent conditions and go on to cause other events. In this respect, causality is ubiquitous and a necessary condition for anything to exist. As McMullen (1996) writes:

> Any situation in the world is continuous with certain other situations in that it flows out of some and helps give rise to others. New qualities of things come into being, other qualities cease to be. To perceive this continuity between spatio-temporal complexes is to appreciate that whatever occurs, occurs under conditions and is itself a condition for the occurrence of other things. This is the core of determinism. Nothing occurs without conditions, without prior events which give rise to it... The actions of human beings then, like anything else, are subject to conditions of occurrence and are themselves conditions of other occurrences.
>
> (p. 65)

This view, however, is not to be confused with proposing simple cause-and-effect chains, or genetic determinism, or the view that psychological processes are some-how causally irrelevant to explanations of behaviour. Instead, causality is best understood as a dynamic network involving causes and effects occurring within a *causal field* ("a background against which the causing goes on"—Mackie, 1974, p. 63).[11] As Mackay and Petocz (2011) write, "this means that the conditions under which an event produces another includes a range of events or situations, a field, and the causal relation may not obtain in a different field" (p. 39). A spark, for instance, will cause a particular gas to combust in one causal field (where, say, oxygen is present) and not in another (where, for instance, oxygen is absent). Closer to psychology, the concept of the causal field is directly relevant to determining whether therapy will be effective. Since each person entering therapy constitutes their own causal field, the potential for therapy to be influential (i.e., to cause therapeutic change) depends also upon each individual. Given the differences in causal fields, psychotherapy might thus be effective for one person but not for another. Accordingly, acknowledging the causal field helps address why different people may respond to the same event differently.

Description and explanation within theories of trauma and dissociation

The use of the term "dissociation" may be especially prone to verbal magic given that the term is used both in a descriptive sense (i.e., as the clinical phenomena to be explained), and in an explanatory sense to account for how symptoms arise (see Cardeña, 1994; Cardeña & Gleaves, 2007). The meaning of the term thus requires careful consideration. On the one hand, if "dissociation" simply means "lack of integration", then dissociation simply re-describes what requires explanation. The standard definition of dissociation is thus *prima facie* unsuitable as an explanatory term. On the other hand, if dissociation is to explain dissociative symptoms, then the term needs to somehow stand logically independent of this "failure of integration". In other words, if dissociation is to serve as a coherent explanatory term, it must be characterised independently of the effects it is said to cause. The nature of "trauma" and "traumatising event" similarly requires careful consideration concerning what it is that stands in the traumatising causal relation that leads to dissociation. As will be later shown, the causal field is particularly important here for understanding why one person might become traumatised after an event and another not.

Making sense of psychological processes

The concept of relation also helps clarify the nature of psychological processes and the relationship between mind and body. There are, of course, many theories concerning the nature of mind and the relationship between mind and body (see, for instance, Brakel, 2013 and Meissner, 2003 for reviews). The approach put forward here is a non-reductionist, realist, materialist approach to mind, which situates both mind and body within the one and the same spatio-temporal universe and yet treats them as logically distinct occurrences (see Anderson, 1962; Maze, 1983; Michell, 1988). Without wishing to trivialise what is necessarily an extremely complicated topic, the thesis here is that it is possible to advance a non-dualist materialist approach to mind, without reducing the mental to materiality. This is achievable by viewing psychological processes as specific *relational acts* occurring between the an individual's brain/perceptual system and various states of affairs in the world. As certain relations, psychological acts cannot be reduced to the body (or parts of the body such as synapses, etc.) even if bodily states are necessary conditions for such psychological acts to occur.[12]

This position means conceptualising the mind not as a thing, but as the brain's (psychological) activities, a view that helps address the ontological status of the mind. As Brenner (1980) writes, "[m]ind is but an aspect of brain functioning, quite as much as respiration is of pulmonary and diaphragmatic functioning or circulation is of cardiac functioning" (p. 206). In this respect, the mind, if anything, is an *activity* of the brain, and even if the brain is a necessary condition for psychological acts, these same activities are not reducible to them. The ontological distinction then is between an *entity* (the brain, etc.) and its *activities*, both existing in the same spatio-temporal universe but nevertheless logically distinct from one another.

The brain, of course, performs many activities, not all of which would be described as "psychological" acts. For instance, some aspects of brain functioning are instead describable as simply physical activities rather than psychological ones (e.g., neuronal activity and changes in brain oxygenation), even if those same activities constitute necessary conditions for whatever we take to mean a psychological act. Addressing what constitutes a psychological act requires clarifying the distinction between what makes an activity a psychological one as opposed to a non-psychological one. Here Franz Brentano's (1874) characterisation of "psychological acts" as *Intentional* activities is a useful starting point for discussing psychological processes. *Intentionality* is accepted by many as the defining criterion of mentality (e.g., Searle, 2004; Solms, 2013), including by some proponents of the structural theory of dissociation (e.g., Nijenhuis, 2015). For Brentano, psychological activities such as believing, thinking, remembering, wishing, and desiring "intend" or are directed towards objects such that when someone knows, believes, desires, or even dreams, there is an "object" of cognition (the something believed, desired, or dreamt of; Brentano, 1874). This "aboutness" or "ofness" of mental acts then means that a person does not simply believe or desire, but rather believes that *x*, or desires that *y*. As Brentano (1874) writes:

> Every mental phenomenon includes something as an object within itself, although they do not do so in the same way. In presentation something is presented, in judgement something is affirmed or denied, in love loved, in hate hated, in desire desired and so on… No physical object exhibits anything like it. We can, therefore, define mental phenomena by saying that they are those which contain an object intentionally within themselves.
>
> (pp. 88–89)

That a person judges *x*, loves *y*, or desires *z*, points to a relational structure of mentality where, more generally, cognition can be taken to involve a relation between a knower (the subject term of the knowing relation) and the situation known (the object term of the knowing relation). As a relation, cognition cannot be reduced to either the cognising subject (the knower) or the known state of affairs.[13] The specific nature of this relation can be broadly described as "knowing": "psychological processes are … typified by a kind of relation not to be found in merely physical interactions, and that is the relation of *knowing about* or *referring to*" (Maze, 1983, p. 83, his italics; cf. Maze & Henry, 1996, p. 1089). Such acts of knowing, in turn, implicate an engaged and motivated mind, as Passmore (in Anderson, 1962) observes:

> [Knowing]…is never … the bare reception of a given object by an act of aware-ness. Rather, it is an attempt to come to terms with ourselves (in self-knowledge) or the things around us … In any adequate theory of knowledge the knowing mind must be regarded as a complex entity with its own demands, which are partly satisfied by, partly encounter obstacles in, the complex behaviour of other things, including other people and other tendencies within the same mind.
>
> (p. xiii)

The argument for Passmore's claim above requires further articulation, and a case will be made in the following chapters that cognition involves not only the brain/ nervous and perceptual systems but also motivational and affective ones.

The knower and the known

On the logic developed earlier, proposing that cognition is a relation between a cognising subject (the knower) and an object term (the known) requires that each term exists independently of the act of knowing. As Anderson (1962) points out, since nothing can be constituted by its relations, "what knows, as well as what is known, must have a character of its own and cannot be defined by its relation to something else" (p. 69). Consequently, given that knowing involves both a know-ing *subject* S and the something known (*p*), then the relation of S's knowing *p* cannot be reduced to either the knower or the known alone. As Anderson writes:

> Knowledge being taken as a relation, it is thus asserted that, when I know this paper, "I know" in no way constitutes this paper, nor does "know this paper" in any way constitute me, nor does "know" constitute either me or this paper.
>
> (p. 27)

Being *known* itself is a specific relationship entered into, and not a property of things, and since any discussion of knowing implicates *both* a knower and a situation known, cognition cannot be reduced to either one of the terms of the relationship.

Given that the terms of the knowing relation are logically independent from the act of knowing, then the subject term (the knower) must have its own intrinsic properties to stand in the knowing relation. What any knower might specifically be is addressed later in Chapter 5, but suffice it here to say that the subject might generally be taken to be the living organism, or more specifically the brain (or some part thereof). As discussed above, however, although neural processes may constitute one term (or part thereof) of the cognitive relation (i.e., the knower), the cognitive relation is not reducible to these. At the same time, although psychologi-cal relations cannot be reduced to physical entities, this is not to say that they then exist in some type of Cartesian mental universe. Just as spatial relations exist in the same spatio-temporal universe as the things standing in those same relationships, so, too, do psychological relations:

> there is no suggestion that the psychological and the physical are distinct realms of existence. They are simply different kinds of events. They both exist and interact in the same spatiotemporal order. In the same way social relations and phenomena are not reducible to either psychological or physical phenomena.
>
> (Michell, 1988, pp. 237–238)

Knowing our own mental processes and the nature of the unconscious

Searle (2004) writes that "[t]he notion of the unconscious is one of the most confused and ill-thought-out conceptions of modern intellectual life. Yet it seems we cannot get on without it" (p. 256). Part of the problem here is that mentality is still often equated with consciousness, making "unconscious mentality" an oxymoron (Searle, 1992; 2004; Talvitie, 2009, 2015). Brentano (1874), for his part, rejected the possibility of unconscious mental acts on the basis that psychological acts were Intentional and so required, at least, some awareness or consciousness of the object cognised. Accordingly, if mental processes are necessarily Intentional (i.e., conscious of something) then an *unconscious* mental process appears to imply an oxymoronic non-Intentional mental state: "An unconscious mental state is exactly like a conscious mental state only minus the consciousness" (Searle, 2004, p. 238). Consequently, argues Searle, since Intentionality means that mental acts necessarily involve awareness, and unconscious processes by definition do not involve awareness, we have then, a paradox:

> Once one adopts the view that mental states are both *in themselves* mental and *in themselves* unconscious, then it is not going to be easy to explain how consciousness fits into the picture. It looks as if the view that mental states are unconscious in themselves has the consequence that consciousness is totally extrinsic, not an essential part of any conscious state or event.
>
> (Searle, 1992, p. 170, his italics; cf. Searle, 2004, pp. 238–239)

While in some ways both Brentano and Searle are correct, this paradox is only apparent. Avoiding this apparent paradox requires appreciating the distinction between *knowing* something and *knowing that, that something is* known. This distinction is found within various accounts described as first- and second-order knowledge (e.g., Brakel, 2010) or between cognition and metacognition (Metcalfe & Shimamura, 1994). The evidence also makes clear that it is possible to know something without knowing that you know it, as seen in various neuroclinical phenomena (e.g., Korsakoff's syndrome, Alzheimer's dementia, split-brain procedures). What such phenomena have in common is that they all demonstrate a distinction between what an individual knows, and what they are capable of reflecting upon (Erdelyi, 1986, 2004; Kihlstrom, 1987).

One implication from the above is that coming to know our own cognitive acts must involve a second mental act, independent of the primary one known. We all, for instance, generally hold the belief that the earth is round, but for the most part we are not currently aware of holding this belief. Moreover, even if a person is not currently aware of holding any such beliefs, it nevertheless makes sense to say that such beliefs are still currently believed, despite not presently being the object of awareness. As Armstrong (1973) points out,

> it is perfectly intelligible to attribute a belief to somebody although there is no relevant vivid idea in his consciousness. We can, for instance, intelligibly attribute a current belief that the earth is round to a man who is sleeping dreamlessly or is unconscious.
>
> (Armstrong, 1973, p. 7)

At the same time, we typically become conscious of holding a belief via an act of reflection. This act of reflection constitutes a secondary mental act, reflecting upon the initial primary one. In fact, given that any mental act must logically exist prior to any reflection upon it, all mental acts begin unconsciously (i.e., unreflected upon) (cf. Freud, 1912g). Thus, on the relational view, when S knows (or wishes, etc.) that p, the relation of knowing (or wishing, etc.) (SRp) is itself unconscious and does not become conscious unless it becomes the object of a second mental act such that S knows SRp.[14] Thus, the distinction between conscious acts that know, and ones that are known means that unconscious mentality is not only defensible but also logically necessary (see Boag, 2012). Consequently, since at any moment we have numerous beliefs, memories (etc.) which we are not currently aware of, most of our mental acts exist unconsciously (cf. Freud, 1912g, 1915e).

The knower and the known in dissociation

Since cognition implicates something standing as the knower (i.e., at least one knowing "subject" term), an important consideration here for later discussion of DID concerns what stands then as the subject term(s). Substantiating what these parts might be, and how they operate, is thus necessary for addressing the question as to whether the dissociative parts "be considered as metaphors for differing emotional states or as genuine entities that have their own memory or identity, which are truly autonomous, and are therefore capable of willful action" (Merkelbach et al., 2002, p. 482). In the former sense, a single subject term thinks erroneously in terms of being multiple knowers, and in the latter, there are actually multiple knowers, each with their own particular points of view.

One factor that complicates answering the question above is that it is not always clear what is meant by "consciousness" in accounts of dissociation. Take, for example, Putnam (1992), who discusses DID in terms of "discrete states of consciousness" (p. 97). As raised in the introduction, Putnam rejects the view that the dissociative parts are independent knowers. If this is the case, then a discrete state of consciousness might be taken then to mean that consciousness is a relation (where, say, S is conscious of y). However, as also previously noted, Putnam also invokes a room metaphor whereby "[t]he alters exist together as a 'family' and differentiate themselves from yet another set of alters that dwell in the 'other room'" (p. 100). This latter sense of consciousness appears to suggest then that there is a variety of independent knowers that are somehow able to differentiate themselves from one another. Whatever the case here specifically is, dissociation is sometimes described either in terms of referring to altered states of consciousness (e.g., Dell, 2009) or with respect to multiple centres of consciousness (e.g., Van der Hart et all., 2006). The former position implies that dissociation involves some specific type of psychological relation, whereby some subject S *experiences* the world in a dissociative manner (e.g., attending to x while ignoring y). The latter position implies that "consciousness" is one of the terms standing in the conscious relation (i.e., consciousness is the knowing subject).

This discussion is directly relevant to the structural theory of dissociation. According to this position, each dissociative part has their own first-person perspective and experience of a separate sense of selfhood (Nijenhuis, 2012, 2015; Van der Hart et al., 2006). Furthermore, each dissociated part has their own thoughts, memories, and so on (e.g., Van der Hart et al., 2006). These dissociated parts of personality thus constitute *knowing subjects* engaging in cognitive activities. Given the logic of relations, each of these knowing subjects must thus be logically independent of both what is known and the cognitive relation itself. This means that each knowing subject must have its own intrinsic qualities and be capable of standing in a cognitive relation to other events. Whether the structural theory adequately address this will be addressed in Chapters 5 and 6. For the time being, it need only be stated here that there is no logical difficulty with postulating multiple knowers within the same individual if these can be stipulated logically independently from one another and from what is known (see Boag, 2005).

Determinism and agency

Addressing dissociative parts also raises questions with respect to agency. Here Martin, Sugarman and Thompson (2003) write that

> *agency*... refers to the deliberative, reflecting activity of a human being in selecting, framing, choosing, and executing his or her actions in a way that is not fully determined by factors and conditions other than his or her own understanding and reasoning.
>
> (p. 112, their italics)

Although possessing a sense of agency is part of human experience, there are some important considerations concerning the causes of human action. "Choosing" cannot be literally "free", if "free" is taken here to mean that under identical causal circumstances different choices and courses of behaviour are possible (cf. William James's (1884) example of the decision to either walk down Divinity Avenue or Oxford Street, "everything else being the same" (p. 30)). Although some still entertain the possibility of such strict free will (see Kane, 2002), the position here is that if identical causal antecedents obtain, then so do identical effects. Humans, of course, do *appear* to choose between courses of actions (cf. Maze, 1983) but that such choice is illusory is backed up by studies indicating that it is possible to manipulate the illusion of free will (Wegner & Wheatley, 1999). In this respect, one task then for psychology is to explain any apparent choice in terms of causal antecedents (Wise, 2004), some of which presumably include unconscious sources of motivation and cognition.[15]

Teleology and determinism

One final topic that requires a word of clarification for addressing dissociation in later chapters and one that is related to the discussion above concerns teleological explanations. Teleological explanations entail a *telos* (an "end" or "purpose") which acts as a final cause for explaining or partially explaining why something occurs (see Audi, 1995). Teleological explanations rest upon the premise that an end-state (an effect) is somehow causally efficacious for bringing something about. Applied to human affairs, teleology is typically bound up with the view that human agency is goal-directed, intentional, and purposeful. Teleological explanations of purposive action generally take the form of an agent performing *A in order to bring about B* (where *B* is some future state of affairs) (see Rychlak, 2000). Humans, of course, do desire states of affairs and such desires appear to be at least partly relevant to explaining what we as humans do when acting purposefully. Nevertheless, it cannot literally be the case that future events—events that have not as yet occurred and may never occur—can be causally relevant to explaining events. As Mackay (1996) notes, "[t]eleological explanations breach the conditions for explanations; they treat the causes of current actions as goals, states which have not yet come about and indeed may never come about" (p. 10). If anything, the *telos* is an effect to be explained, and so as Wise (2004) recognises, "[t]he apparent goal direction of motivated behaviour explains nothing; it is the mystery that remains to be explained" (p. 160). What we instead need to know is how the causal antecedents work together to produce the effects that we wish to explain. As Waelder (1960) writes, "[w]ithout such explanations of 'how it works,' teleological explanations explain nothing; they merely add to a description of a process the information that it is useful for a purpose, implying that its existence is due to its usefulness" (p. 171).

Nevertheless, any coherent theory must account for apparent teleology, and purpose and goal-directedness can sometimes be accounted for in a manner consistent with efficient causality by adopting a teleonomic approach (from Pittendrigh, 1958; see Thompson, 1987; Mayr, 1974). Teleonomic explanations are strictly causal and mechanistic: apparent goal-directed behaviour is initiated by mechanisms (or what Mayr (1974) broadly calls "programs") such that any "teleonomic" system, "living or mechanical, … is so constructed that, when activated in its environment of adaptedness, it achieves a predictable outcome" (Bowlby, 1969, p. 139). Considering feedback processes, one can attribute apparent goal-directedness to both living systems and machines (such as with a guided missile), and thus making apparent goal-directedness consistent with a deterministic psychology (Bowlby, 1969).[16] Moreover, although nothing occurs without conditions, human factors are just as much part of the causal fabric as anything else. This means that cognitive acts, including believing and planning, are not incommensurable with determinism since there is no logical objection to postulating such processes as causal antecedents involved in apparent goal-directed activity (Maze, 1983; Michell, 1988). The common-sense (or folk-psychological) model explains behaviour in such a manner, whereby a "desire" provides the motivation for behaviour while the "belief" (which includes believing, planning, etc.) plays an instrumental role with respect to guiding the desire. More formally, when explaining person P's doing A, we posit both that (i) P desires B; and (ii) P believes that doing A leads to B. To take a simple example from Wollheim (1991), an act of drinking is explicable with respect to both a desire to drink and a belief that water will satisfy that desire. Such cognitive acts are themselves caused, however, and simply constitute part of the wider causal circumstances leading to effects. Consequently, embracing determinism and denying teleology is not to deny a role for human consciousness, fore-thought, planning, and so on.

As will be discussed in Chapter 4, the topic of teleology is particularly relevant to accounts invoking "purpose" to explain dissociation. Purpose is particularly prominent in teleological defence accounts whereby dissociation occurs in order to protect the individual. For example, in the context of defensive dissociation, Howell and Itzkowitz (2016a) write that the "very purpose" of dissociation is "to keep the person living in a world of partial truths, confusion caused by gaps in experience, and shifting dissociated self-states" (p. 16). Nevertheless, it is sometimes possible to re-read teleological explanations in terms of causal antecedents. As such, whether any theory of defensive dissociation can be re-cast in terms of efficient causality remains to be seen.

This notwithstanding, discussing dissociation in purposive terms raises questions with respect to how such dissociation specifically occurs. For example, according to Braude (2014), rather than arising from any accidental occurrence, "true" dissociation is such that "x and y are separated by a phenomenological or epistemological barrier (e.g., amnesia, anaesthesia) erected by S" (p. 32). Braude stipulates this condition since he views dissociation as a defensive activity undertaken by the agent S. This position may be fair enough, but there are, however, several challenges associated then with explaining such dissociation. For example, if such barriers are to mean anything more than simply pseudo-explanatory metaphors, it is necessary then to address what the barrier specifically consists of and how it is maintained. The subject S performing this act also needs to be accounted for, as well as explaining how this agent S could erect such a barrier without it being self-defeating. In this latter respect, the specific problem here is that erecting any such a barrier between say x and y would presumably require somehow knowing both x and y in the first place. To say this all occurs unconsciously, as Braude claims, is not unreasonable, but this still does not address how the process occurs, including how awareness of the act itself is prevented from conscious recognition. Consequently, any such defensive account of dissociation requires a coherent mechanism for successfully explaining how such dissociation could coherently occur. Addressing such questions is more than simply a theoretical concern, since as Braude (2014) observes, meeting this challenge is also clinically relevant for addressing the reversibility of dissociation. Accordingly, theories of defensive dissociation need to pass the logical test if they are to stand as potential explanations of dissociative pathology.

Summary

This chapter puts forward a realist conceptual framework to provide criteria for judging the coherency of theories of trauma and dissociation. As developed above, a range of theoretical and conceptual considerations are relevant to making sense of dissociation. The concept of relation is critically important because dissociation is itself a form of relation, and so the terms of the dissociative relationship require clarification. Psychological processes can also be seen as certain relations, and clarifying the subject and object terms of the dissociative relation is important for addressing the knower in accounts of DID. It is also important to avoid reification and circular explanation, both of which occur when the concept of relations is neglected. Description is also logically distinct from explanation, and determining whether dissociation is primarily a descriptive of explanatory term depends upon different theoretical perspectives. Causality as a relation additionally requires that causes and effects be logically distinct, and that causes precede effects. As such, apparent teleology as found in purposive accounts of dissociative defence need to be recast in terms of causal antecedents. As will be demonstrated in the following chapters, these considerations provide useful conceptual tools for assessing claims concerning trauma-dissociation and the two major approaches to explaining dissociation, the Janetian and Freudian perspectives.

Notes

1 As discussed elsewhere (Boag, 2017), the term "metaphysics" is construed variously (see van Inwagen & Zimmerman, 2008) but is commonly associated with the Kantian-derived viewpoint whereby "[m]etaphysics concerns ultimate reality" (Talvitie & Ihanus, 2011, p. 1588). This narrow metaphysical position assumes that we can never directly access an unknowable, "ultimate" reality lying beyond experience. By implication then, we cannot make objective knowledge claims about this reality (see Hibberd, 2014). Nevertheless, such a position cannot be coherently maintained without being self-contradictory, given that the claim itself is put forward as an objective knowledge claim concerning reality (Maze, 2001).

2 The realist position employed here is associated with a particular Australian school of realism (see Baker, 1986) and developed more recently as "situational realism" by Hibberd (2014).

3 Such realism, as proposed here, does not mean, however, that we cannot be in error. Factual knowledge is a hard-fought achievement given the obstacles to discovery including various biases and limitations of our perceptual system.

4 As Braude (2014) points out, this dissociation need not be symmetrical however (i.e., *y* may or may not be dissociated from *x*), but this does not detract from the basic point here that both terms are logically independent of one another.

5 "Ontology" "is the science of what is, of the kinds and structures of objects, properties, events, processes, and relations in every area of reality" (Smith, 2003, p. 155).

6 "Terms" are what stand in relationship to one another, rather than simply referring to linguistic entities (unless specifically addressing aspects of language).

7 Logical independence does not prevent the possibility of internal relations within complex entities and situations, since the parts internal to any entity can, of course, stand in relationship to one another and other situations (Maze, 1983). We can, for instance, speak sensibly of the relation, say, between heart and brain, each existing within one and same body. Nevertheless, any internal part must be logically independent of any other part it is said to stand in relation to.

8 It is important to note the conditional "If" here. If amnesia means something distinct from "not being able to remember", then amnesia might serve as a useful explanatory term (i.e., if "amnesia" is logically distinct from not being able to remember).

9 It might be objected here that any such "ability" might simply act as a placeholder for a set of causal factors that explain the performance. If so, then the "ability" becomes redundant once we have identified these specific causal influences (see Boag, 2018).

10 The problem with reification and circular explanation is also apparent in Faculty psychology approaches to explanation, a position found within Aristotelian philosophy, and prominent in medieval Scholasticism (O'Neil, 1982). The Faculty approach entails explaining an event's occurrence by postulating a "faculty", "power", or "force" that brings the effect into being. The Scholastics, for instance, postulated a "pulsific faculty" for explaining the heart's beating (Clarke, 1989), and the Scottish philosopher Thomas Reid "explained" moral reasoning and behaviour with respect to a "moral faculty" (Reid, 1785/1970). The problem with such Faculties is that they are identified from the event to be explained and conceptually bound to that which they were attempting to account for (see Passmore, 1935 for further discussion).

11 Further discussion of causal fields can be found in Baker (1986, chapter 8) and White's (1990) discussion of "causal frames" (p. 14).

12 I would like to thank Erik Reichle here for recommending Max Coltheart's 2012 paper arguing against reductionism (Coltheart, 2012).

13 The objects of cognition can be described as *propositional*, given that what is known are objective situations, occurrences, events, or states of affairs (Maze, 1983; Michell, 1988). As Michell (1988) writes: "A situation is always a matter of *something's being of a certain kind* or of *something's being related in a particular way to other things*, and so its structure is propositional (i.e., of the subject-predicate form)" (pp. 233–234, his italics).

14 On the other hand, just as "awareness" is a relationship, it can also be seen that to be "being unaware" (or ignorant) is also to be "unaware" or ignorant *of something*, and so, too, a relation between a subject and some state of affair. If ignorance is a relation, then we can also, of course, be ignorant of our own ignorance (Michell, 1988; Nisbett & Wilson, 1977).

15 If humans could act independently of (or in violation to) those causes—then it would mean that human decisions could somehow violate the fabric of the universe itself: it would be "in principle possible for an organism to cut across, to suspend, whatever mechanical forces might be operating (inside or outside it) to bring about its behaviour" (McMullen, 1982, pp. 226–227). This notwithstanding, how any act of will literally arises from nothing is impossible to comprehend: such free will would have to be "literally independent of material causes, arising *de novo* from some unconditional source such as a spontaneous act of will" (McMullen, 1996, p. 65). Consequently, without a deterministic outlook, the scientific study of any phenomenon would be impossible, since random, non-causal fluctuations could pervade any field of research (see Maze, 1983, 1987).

16 As argued elsewhere, Freud's general metapsychology explains apparent goal-directed human activity in such a teleonomic manner (Boag, 2017).

Chapter 3

Does trauma cause dissociation?

Having outlined a conceptual framework for evaluating theories of trauma-dissociation, the first step here for assessing trauma-dissociation is to consider the causal claim that trauma causes dissociation. To address such a claim requires a clear understanding of what is meant by "trauma" and traumatisation, which, at first glance, might seem straightforward: terrifying events instigate overwhelming emotions such as intense fear, which, in turn, lead to long-term personality disturbances and disruptions in functioning. However, the situation is not so clear cut since there is a lack of clarity concerning the term trauma. As Weathers and Keane (2008) note, although "[t]rauma is a fundamental concept in the field of traumatic stress, ... it is difficult to define and has been the source of much controversy" (p. 657). Moreover, conceptualisations of "trauma" have both evolved and multiplied (Jones & Wessely, 2006), with Howell and Itzkowitz (2016c) noting that "[t]he word "trauma" is used in multifarious ways to refer to many different kinds of experiences" (p. 33). Here, one finds that various theoretical perspectives conceptualise trauma differently (e.g., psychodynamic vs behavioural traditions—Dalenberg, Straus & Carlson, 2017). Moreover, there are also specific types of traumas, including betrayal trauma (Gobin & Freyd, 2014), developmental trauma (Denton et al., 2017), massive trauma (Danieli, 2009), cumulative trauma (Hodges et al., 2013), intergenerational trauma (Bombay, Matheson & Anisman, 2009), social trauma (Hamburger, 2021), and so on.

The term "trauma" itself finds its roots in Greek, meaning "wound" (Laplanche & Pontalis, 1974; Schimmenti, 2018). Originally denoting physical injuries, the term was metaphorically extended in the 19th century to encompass psychological ones. Such wounds involve relatively enduring effects: "[t]rauma ... always seems to involve a permanent after-effect of some sort ("something is left behind")" (Sandler et al., 1991, p. 139). In this respect, trauma appears critical for understanding DID given the extensive evidence that adverse childhood events appear to underlie pathological dissociation (Bailey & Brand, 2017; Dalenberg et al., 2012, 2014; Raison & Andrea, 2023; Reinders & Veltman, 2021; Şar, Dorahy & Krüger, 2017). As Dorahy et al. (2014) summarise, "*[e]very study that has systematically examined aetiology has found that antecedent severe, chronic childhood trauma is present in the histories of almost all individuals with DID*" (p. 408, italics in original).

DOI: 10.4324/9781003328254-3

At the same time, if trauma means wound, then it would not make sense to say that trauma causes "injury" because they are one and the same (i.e., the claim would be circular), even if secondary problems might follow (e.g., infection, as in the case of a physical injury). Nevertheless, it is not uncommon to see the claim that trauma is not an injury per se, but instead a cause of injury, as seen in Schimmenti and Caretti's (2016) claim that "trauma causes injury to the mind and its inherent functions and processes, including the ego, identity, and self-structure" (p. 108). Here, the meaning of trauma shifts from the impact upon the person to the event causing the impact. If it is the case that trauma acts as a cause of psychopathology and dissociation, then "trauma" needs to be logically independent of the same effect that it is said to cause. However, this independence is not always clear, since the concept of trauma sometimes refers both to the event and the impact upon the individual. Consider, for instance, Howell and Itzkowitz's (2016c) claim that "the result of trauma is dissociation" (cf. Howell, 2005, p. vii), and then later that "[t]rauma then connotes divisions or fissures in experience" (p. 35). In the former sense, trauma appears to be a cause of dissociation, while in the latter sense, the meaning of trauma appears to imply the dissociative effect upon the person.

Since causes and effects need to be logically independent, trauma cannot both be causes and effect without succumbing to circularity. However, at the outset, we are confronted with conceptual ambiguity: the term psychological trauma is used sometimes to refer to an event, or to an individual's subjective appraisal of the event, or to the acute and chronic distress that follows, or all of these together (Sandler et al., 1991; Weathers & Keane, 2008; Zepf & Zepf, 2008). As developed earlier, Zepf and Zepf (2008) accordingly summarise,

> there is often no distinction made … as to whether trauma is thought of as the event itself or the experience of it. At times trauma is regarded as the process of traumatization, the traumatic state, and at other times it refers to the permanent subsidiary changes in the affected subject.
>
> (p. 331)

As developed in the introduction, resolving this is not likely to be helped by simply appealing to the empirical evidence given that the crux of the problem here is conceptual. This means that whether trauma is a satisfactory explanation for dissociation requires fresh consideration.

The aim of this chapter is to examine the concept of trauma in order to assess the trauma-dissociation link. The chapter first traces the shift of trauma from injury to event, by discussing the origin of the conceptualisation of trauma in modern psychology and subsequent problems associated with the codification of trauma in diagnostic systems. The chapter then develops a relational view of traumatisation and outlines conceptual difficulties associated with proposing that trauma causes dissociation. Requirements for explanations of traumatisation are then considered, before addressing the view that traumatisation should be understood as a process.

As a process, the chapter identifies some minimum requirements that any theory of trauma-dissociation must satisfy to provide a foundation for later addressing the major theories of trauma-dissociation found today.

Traumatisation and traumatic events

The modern meaning of trauma finds its roots in the observation of shell shock victims in the First World War (Myers, 1915; Turner, 1915). Trauma there was defined in terms of psychic, nervous, or mental "shock" with the primary determinant of the shock being attributed to the experience of shelling (Loughran, 2012). Turner (1915) observed that soldiers exposed to sustained artillery fire and enduring prolonged fatigue and exhaustion would manifest a range of symptoms including concussion, amnesia, states of confusion, somatoform symptoms, and exhaustion. Although not all of the original cases of shell shock would qualify now as posttraumatic stress disorder (PTSD) (Loughran, 2012), many cases would, as reflected in the two traumatisation syndromes that typically emerged: some individual would become dazed, apathetic, and lethargic, and seemingly unresponsive to their surroundings, while others became fearful and easily startled: "In some cases the patient would appear to be living again through an experience of the past, probably associated with the time of onset of the symptoms" (Turner, 1915, p. 833). These two sets of symptoms represent precursors of the current understanding of PTSD (Langer, 2013; Ozer et al., 2003). PTSD itself only first formally emerged in DSM-III (American Psychiatric Association, 1980) (Langer, 2013; Ozer et al., 2003) and was initially classified as an anxiety disorder in response to a "recognizable stressor that would evoke significant symptoms of distress in almost everyone" (APA, 1980, p. 238). The stressor was such that it evoked intense fear, terror, and helplessness, which acted as a cause of intrusive re-experiencing of the traumatising event (e.g., flashbacks and nightmares), avoidance and numbing symptoms (e.g., avoiding certain thoughts and forgetting important aspects of the event), as well as hyperarousal (e.g., difficulty sleeping or being easily startled).

Although these core symptoms of PTSD have remained relatively stable throughout the various DSM revisions, the conceptualisation of traumatising events (i.e., what qualifies as possible traumata) has undergone various revisions with each subsequent DSM.[1] Traumatic stressors in DSM-III were ones outside the "normal range of experiences" and included events involving exposure to threat to life/physical integrity (for self or family), natural disasters, car accidents, war, rape, and torture. DSM-III-R later extended traumatising events to include witnessing and learning about a traumatic event (APA, 1987), while DSM-IV (APA, 1994) added developmentally inappropriate experiences without threatened violence or injury. DSM-5, in turn, allowed the possibility of PTSD resulting from "[f]irst-hand repeated or extreme exposure to aversive details of the traumatic event (not through media, pictures, television or movies unless work-related)", as with emergency service personnel who are regularly exposed to distressing events (APA, 2013, p. 271). This expansion of possible traumatic events has, in turn, been extensively criticised, with several critics seizing upon the widening classes of possible traumata as conceptual "bracket creep" (Haslam, 2016; McNally, 2003b, 2007, 2010): whereas life-threatening events initially qualified as traumatic stress-ors, now non-life-threatening events could also meet diagnostic threshold (e.g., infidelity, suddenly moving home—Haslam, 2016). Critics note that such bracket creep could easily lead to PTSD being overly diagnosed (Baes et al., 2023), as well as trivialised. In the latter instance, if ostensibly minor events can count as traumatic stressors, then nearly everyone counts as a trauma-survivor (McNally, 2003b, 2010).

Haslam (2016) does, however, also recognise that such conceptual creep is not necessarily negative and may even be appropriate. He writes, "[c]onceptual revi-sion is to be expected in view of changing scientific and social realities, and it may be appropriately responsive to those changes" (p. 2). However, the underlying issue here is the emphasis on categorising events as traumatising (i.e., DSM Criterion A), an issue that Dalenberg et al. (2017) note is a probable consequence of attempting to establish an objective definition of trauma to create reliable and valid diagnosis of PTSD. In turn, the Criterion A approach to trauma has meant that "the field of traumatology has in effect equated the term with the probability of an event causing PTSD" (Dalenberg et al., 2017; p. 22). Thus, the concept of "trauma" has increas-ingly been associated with events that lead to PTSD, regardless of their impact on individuals. Consider, for instance, McNally's (2003a) claim that, "[e]xposure to trauma is common, but PTSD is relatively rare" (p. 779). McNally's observation implies that an event can be considered traumatic even if no one is traumatised.

Conceptualising trauma as an event further necessitates discerning which occur-rences might rightly qualify as "traumatic", and it is not difficult to see here that determining what constitute traumata (i.e., causing distress in almost anyone) will be open to interpretation (Dalenberg et al., 2017).[2] One reason for this is that peo-ple's responses to "traumatising events" are determined by multiple interacting factors (Bryant, 2006; Schimmenti, 2018).[3] Indeed, ample evidence indicates a multifaceted array of risk factors predict PTSD development, including lack of social support, trauma severity, and life stress (Brewin, Andrews & Valentine, 2000). As Putnam (2003), for instance, writes, in connection with CSA:

> The array of disorders and dysfunctional behaviors associated with CSA has been difficult to account for with a simple cause-and-effect model. This appar-ent diversity can be explained in part by the heterogeneity of CSA experiences, the complexity of the confounds among abuse severity variables, and a host of moderating and mediating constitutional and environmental variables together with important individual differences in coping strategies that may come into play at different points in development in any given case.
>
> (Putnam, 2003, p. 273)

The ongoing interaction of factors is especially apparent with "complex trauma", whereby recurring adverse interpersonal events experienced at developmentally vulnerable periods interact to shape psychopathological outcomes:

> The traumatic stress field has adopted the term "complex trauma" to describe the experience of multiple, chronic and prolonged, developmentally adverse traumatic events, most often of an interpersonal nature (e.g., sexual or physical abuse, war, community violence) and early-life onset. These exposures often occur within the child's caregiving system and include physical, emotional, and educational neglect and child maltreatment beginning in early childhood.
>
> (Van der Kolk, 2005, p. 402)

What this all points to is that understanding traumatisation necessarily requires considering a complex set of person and situational factors that are relevant for understanding how people react to extremely stressful events. Given such complexity, it is too simplistic to say that "catastrophic" life events such as combat, sexual assault, and natural disasters should only qualify as "traumatic", even if some events are more likely than others to evoke "traumatic stress". Consequently, it makes little sense to search for an objective criteria list of traumata: one can only say what is more or less likely to be traumatising based on previous evidence and theory. As such, the bracket creep problem described earlier follows from defining trauma in relation to the stressor, when the real problem facing trauma researchers is addressing the inherent complexity involved in traumatisation.

The view that "trauma" is not simply an event is already well-recognised amongst dissociation researchers. Van der Hart et al. (2006), for example, write that "events are not traumatic in themselves, rather, they may be so in their effects on a given individual" (p. 23). Making sense of the impact here requires understanding the process of traumatisation, which necessitates addressing the relevant systems, their components, and their interactions unfolding across time. As Şar and Ozturk (2006) write:

> Trauma is not limited to or identical with a noxious event. Thus, the term posttraumatic stress disorder is a misleading one. Trauma is, in fact, an experience which is related to both the subjective and objective components of a situation. ... trauma is not merely a situational phenomenon, but a longitudinal socio-psychological process which develops in time and follows a course.
>
> (p. 8)

With respect to the conceptual framework developed in the previous chapter, appreciating the complexity of factors involved means that, if anything, "traumatisation" involves a complex relationship between events and the individuals who experience them, as Zepf and Zepf (2008) recognise:

> Trauma is a binomial, relational concept referring to experiences that combine an external event with its specific consequences for an individual's psychic

reality. It is not the event that is the crucial factor but the manner in which it is experienced and mastered. The definition of an event as traumatic can only be made as a result of the effects it has in the individual's psychic life.

(p. 89)

As such, to speak of traumatisation requires considering the impact of some event E on an individual S, within some causal field C. To reduce "trauma" then to either the event or the person alone is to reify the person-situation traumatising relation.

If the above discussion is accepted, then what this subsequently means is that the claim that "trauma causes dissociation" is logically problematic. This is because the concept of trauma necessarily contains reference to dissociation and so the two terms cannot be logically independent from one another (i.e., trauma cannot be separated from the psychopathological effects upon the individual). Of course, abandoning the claim that "trauma causes dissociation" flies in the face of the apparent evidence that traumatic events do cause dissociative psychopathology (Bailey & Brand, 2017; Dalenberg et al., 2012, 2014; Dorahy et al., 2014; Raison & Andrea, 2023; Reinders & Veltman, 2021; Şar, Dorahy & Krüger, 2017). Moreover, it is possible that the phrase "trauma causes dissociation" is simply shorthand for what is undoubtedly a complex causal state of affairs. Nevertheless, it also appears to be the case that the complexity of the concept of traumatisation is not always clearly appreciated, since trauma is sometimes understood as primarily an event, or as an individual's subjective appraisal of the event, or as the acute and chronic distress that follows (cf. Sandler et al., 1991; Weathers & Keane, 2008; Zepf & Zepf, 2008). Thus, abandoning the claim that "trauma causes dissociation" is only to reject the oversimplistic approach that fails to address the complex process involved in traumatisation.

Addressing the complexity of traumatisation

Avoiding oversimplification requires instead a more nuanced approach that acknowledges the multifaceted nature of traumatisation. One useful approach for addressing the complexity of traumatisation is Harvey's (1996) ecology of trauma model. Ecology is the study of the interrelationship between organisms and their environments, and Harvey recognises that making sense of traumatisation requires addressing what can be broadly described as person, event, and environmental variables. These variables each interact with one another in shaping traumatising responses (Person × Event × Environment), such that a person's(s) experience of an event occurs within a larger context (the "environment"), which includes community, social, cultural, and political factors, each of which is itself complex. As such, traumatisation is not simply a cause-effect relation, but rather entails causes, effects, within a complex causal field. This means that traumatisation emerge from a complex interplay between various developing and unfolding systems, broadly involving the "person" and "culture". With regard to the latter, Kirmayer (2011) observes that traumatisation is also shaped by cultural expectations:

> Trauma itself is not a well-defined or sharply delimited category of experience, but one that brings together diverse situations according to nosological and cultural conventions ... There are many different mechanisms activated when people are exposed to violent, life-threatening or other terrifying situations that may contribute to diverse forms of psychopathology and dissociative experience.
>
> (p. 465)

In this respect, there are clearly cross-cultural variations in PTSD presentation (Marques et al., 2011), as well as variation across history of what would now be described as PTSD (see Jones and Wessely's (2006) historical review).

It is because of this complex interaction of traumatising events, individual differences, and the broader context, that individuals respond in strikingly different ways to what appears to be ostensibly the same event. As Gerhart, Canetti and Hobfoll (2015) write: "the long-term response to trauma is complex and ideographic, with individuals showing unique reactions to the traumatic event based on the unique ecology in which they live" (p. 4). The same event may lead to widely discrepant responses and symptoms amongst individuals, with any two individuals producing differing responses based on their own unique life histories. Consequently, traumatisation and the development of DID include not only the severity, type, and duration of the traumatising stressor but also the developmental stage of the individual, attachment relationships, family dynamics, culture, and so on (cf. Dorahy et al., 2014).

Trauma as process and the relation of traumatisation

The more difficult issue, however, is to account for this process of traumatisation, and although there are established correlations between various risk factors and PTSD, what is less clear is the actual process of how such risk factors conspire to lead to psychopathological outcomes. Addressing the process of traumatisation will be developed further in the next chapter when examining theories of trauma-dissociation. However, it is possible here to first clarify the relational structure of traumatisation further and to help identify which approaches may lead potentially to theoretical dead ends. To illustrate this, consider the proposal that traumatisation in some way "overwhelms" the individual. Van der Kolk (2000), for example, defines trauma in terms of "stress that overwhelms the organism" (p. 13), such that the process of traumatisation involves overwhelming an individual's coping mechanisms or defences. In a parallel vein, Van der Kolk and Fisler (1995) write that "trauma is defined as the experience of an inescapable stressful event that overwhelms one's existing coping mechanisms" (p. 506; cf. Van der Kolk, 1998, p. S52). Follette and Vijay (2009) similarly write: "A traumatic event is considered anything that overwhelms a person's ability to cope and subsequently impedes their ability to function effectively" (p. 300).

This approach to understanding the process of traumatisation might seem reasonable enough: certain events elicit strong emotions that are too intense to master, in turn leading to psychopathological effects. In such a theoretical scheme, the causal relationship can be understood in terms of coping mechanisms (or failure thereof) mediating (or intervening) between the event and the pathological outcome. The causal relationship then is an event that triggers intense emotions, which in turn overwhelms the defensive operations and leads to dissociative pathology (*viz.* triggering event-coping failure-dissociative effects). Nevertheless, as a causal relationship, we need to be able to characterise the terms of the relationship independently of one another, which requires characterising the concept of "being overwhelmed" independently of the dissociative effects. One question here, however, concerns the precise meaning of being "overwhelmed". As will be shown, it is prima facie difficult to characterise the term "overwhelmed" independently of the effects that it is purported to explain. Consider, for instance, the relationship between trauma, being overwhelmed, and dissociation in the following:

> If ... trauma is an inescapably stressful event that overwhelms people's existing coping mechanisms, then it refers to events that were too overwhelming to be assimilated. There is a split in experience. Experience that is too overwhelming to be assimilated will cause a division of experiencing and knowledge.
>
> (Howell & Itzkowitz, 2016c, p. 35)

These authors appear here to be making a causal claim ("Experience that is too overwhelming to be assimilated will *cause* a division of experiencing and knowledge"). At the same time, it is also not altogether clear that the relevant terms are independent of one another. For instance, "being overwhelmed" appear to be essentially the same as both trauma and dissociation since "trauma is an inescapably stressful event that overwhelms", and "events that are too overwhelming cannot be assimilated" (i.e., "overwhelming" is defined in terms of dissociation). Formulated as such, being "overwhelming" is not independent of the effects it is said to explain. Consequently, the term "overwhelming" cannot satisfactorily characterise a process mediating between events and pathological effects because the terms are not logically independent of one another.

A similar problem is seen in Freud's attempt to address traumatisation "economically", whereby traumatisation here involves excitations that were quantitatively too strong to be mastered. Freud writes that "the term 'traumatic' has no other sense than an economic one" (Freud, 1916–1917, p. 275), and unlike the conflict-ridden psychoneuroses (which were, for the most part, the focus of psychoanalysis), "traumatic neuroses" were psychopathological conditions that arose after "frightening experiences or severe accidents, without any reference to a conflict in the ego" (Freud, 1919d, p. 209).[4] Freud (1920g) describes the specific mechanism of traumatisation here in terms of the breaking of a "protective shield":

> We describe as 'traumatic' any excitations from outside which are powerful enough to break through the protective shield. It seems to me that the concept of trauma necessarily implies a connection of this kind with a breach in an otherwise efficacious barrier against stimuli.
>
> (p. 29)

In other words, an individual is ordinarily protected from being overstimulated by psychic energy through a protective barrier. This shield, however, has only a limited capacity to protect, and once that barrier is broken, the individual is "flooded with large amounts of stimulus" (p. 29). This, in turn, leads to an economic overload that interferes with the system's normal functioning.

Freud's protective-shield account might appear to provide a semblance of a potential mechanism for understanding how events that instigate vehement emotional responses might traumatise someone. However, there are several problematic issues here. First, there is no evidence for this "protective shield", apart from with respect to whether it succeeds or fails in protecting the individual from events. As such, attempting to explain traumatisation through a failure of the shield—while also using traumatisation as evidence for the shield—provides a form of circularity: a person is traumatised because their protective shield failed, and the evidence for this claim is simply that the person is traumatised. Of course, we might surmise that independent evidence may nevertheless be forthcoming.[5] However, without knowing what this shield consists of, we have no manner of characterising the breaking of the shield independently from the effects it is said to explain. Thus, the "protective shield" should be treated, at best, as a metaphor for traumatisation, rather than as a serious scientific explanation (cf. Zepf & Zepf, 2008). Consequently, we are still left without a satisfactory account of the traumatising process occurring between events and the individual's response.[6]

Can defence help provide a process of traumatisation?

As developed above, if the term "overwhelming" is to stand as an explanation of dissociation, then it cannot also be defined in reference to dissociative responses. The question then is whether it might be possible to characterise "being overwhelmed" independently from the purported effects that the term is said to explain. One potential avenue here is to view dissociation defensively, whereby dissociation itself occurs as a type of shut-off mechanism that prevents the person from being overwhelmed. For instance, Shore (2009) describes dissociation as "the bottom-line survival defense against overwhelming, unbearable, emotional experiences" (p. 195). In such accounts, dissociation serves a defensive function, which can nevertheless lead to psychopathological outcomes such as dissociative pathology. Schimmenti (2018) similarly, writes that although the defensive function of dissociation is to protect the mind from becoming overwhelmed, when dissociation becomes "overly activated and relied upon as a person's primary response to stress, it can become pathological and may foster psychopathology" (p. 554). In other words, dissociation becomes habit-like when overly relied upon, and so what is originally a self-protective response becomes subsequently pathological.

There might be merit to Schimmenti's approach above since we have good examples of how responses that are initially adaptive can become pathological (e.g., chronic cortisol activation—Knezevic et al. (2023)). Consequently, if defensive responses can be grounded within ordinary psychological functioning and consistent with efficient causality, then there may be a coherent basis for postulating a process of traumatisation, whereby events that instigate terror in turn trigger defensive responses, which in turn lead to dissociative pathology.[7] An example of such an account is found in the proposal that appraisal of extreme threat instigates basic survival responses such as fight/flight/freeze, which subsequently interfere with the initial processing of experiences. This interference, in turn, leads to a chronic dissociative failure of integration (Schauer & Elbert, 2010). Kinniburgh et al. (2005), for example, write:

> Although the term "trauma" describes many types of experiences, common across trauma exposures is the initiation of biologically driven "fight-flight freeze" responses that help the organism survive. Danger activates some physiological resources and de-activates others; processes associated with survival (e.g., rapid motoric activation, arousal) become prioritized over processes associated with higher cognitive functions (e.g., planning, organization, inhibition of response). Among children exposed to intense or repeated traumas, these responses are likely to be triggered by minor stresses, even in response to cues that, objectively, do not signify actual danger.
>
> (pp. 427–428).

The specific mechanism above involves threat appraisal and fight-flight-freeze responses shutting down ordinary emotional processing and the possibility of learning. As a result, certain experiences are thereby never accessible (i.e., are "dissociated") since they were never initially encoded. Schauer and Ellbert (2010) here write that the "[e]xperience of overwhelming threat may interfere with the process of integrating active elements of sensation, emotion, and cognition into the particular declarative memory of the event and thus result in disorders of the trauma spectrum" (p. 109). Although this explanatory strategy would seemingly prevent dissociation being undone, such an approach is nevertheless consistent with linking dissociative defensive response to animal defensive ones (see Nijenhuis, Vanderlinden & Spinhoven, 1998). Their approach has the further advantage of conceptualising responses to extreme threat within an evolutionary framework that is consistent with expected phylogenetic responses.[8] This approach also has the major advantage of providing a potentially suitable explanation given that causes and effects are logically independent: events that evoke threat trigger evolutionarily shaped defensive responses, which in turn impact upon processing mechanisms.

Traumatisation, appraisal, and emotions

Whether such an account helps us to understand traumatisation will be developed later in Chapter 6, but one noteworthy point to take from the above is that traumatisation appears to necessarily involve threat appraisal. In this respect, Ozer et al. (2003) write

> that the psychological aspects of exposure may be the most important, and that the in-the-moment appraisal and meaning of the traumatic stressor may have as much to do with explaining who develops PTSD as do the more static factors such as adjustment, prior exposure, or concurrent psychopathology.
>
> (p. 69)

Van der Kolk and McFarlane (1996) similarly highlight the importance of subjective appraisal and meaning in their discussion of PTSD when they write:

> The critical element that makes an event traumatic is the subjective assessment of the victims of how threatened and helpless they feel. So although the reality of extraordinary events is at the core of PTSD, the meaning that victims attach to these events is as fundamental as the trauma itself. People's interpretations of the meaning of the trauma continue to evolve well after the trauma itself has ceased.
>
> (p. 6)

One result of this, as Weathers and Keane (2007) note, is that the "perception of an event as stressful depends on subjective appraisal, making it difficult to define stressors objectively, and independent of personal meaning making" (p. 108). Additionally, with respect to making sense of traumatisation, threat appraisal implicates both perception and interpretation and, as such, necessarily entails psychological processes (where S appraises some event x as a threat). Traumatisation is then, in some respects, a psychological process.

"Appraisal" must also clearly operate at the psychological level given that detecting threat or any other such evaluation requires *judgement* (see Boag, 2012, 2022). The simple reason for this that being "threatening" is a relation whereby some subject S judges some event x to be a threat, such that although x may be threatening for one person, it may not be so for another (cf. Leising et al., 2009).[9] Given this, it is not possible to outsource this judgement to some type of neural mechanism or other non-psychological process, even if, of course, neural mechanisms may mediate this process (see Boag, 2012).

Clarification is, however, required here with respect to whether such threat detection is conscious or not. As developed in the previous chapter, it is logically possible to believe that x is a threat, without knowing that x is even known, since these are independent mental acts.[10] As such, although threat appraisal requires judging some event as threatening, that judgement itself need not be known, and so can be coherently described as "unconscious threat detection". Moreover, this proposal is backed up by evidence. Rofé (2008), for example, writes that "there seems to be strong evidence for unconscious sensitivity to threatening stimuli" (p. 70), and various mediating neural mechanisms appear to be implicated here (LeDoux, 1990, 1995; LeDoux & Schiller, 2009; Liotti & Panksepp, 2004; Maren & Quirk, 2004; Öhman, 2009).[11] Nevertheless, further clarification is required here since it is easy to treat this sensitivity as something non-psychological. For example, Pugh (2002) writes that the amygdala appears to be "involved in the implicit, unconscious processing of emotion" (p. 1380), whereby fear processing occurs via subcortical processing. Such subcortical processing is commonly taken to involve the absence of person-level "conscious" recognition of the eliciting stimulus (Öhman, Carlsson, Lundqvist & Ingvar, 2007, p. 181) and described in ways that would appear to preclude psychological processes. For example, Öhman (2009) writes that "awareness is not a necessary condition for fear conditioning" (p. 144), suggesting that threat can be detected without even the awareness of the target of threat.

However, as developed above, threat detection necessarily involves some target being perceived and evaluated as a threat. Consequently, such detection cannot be reduced to non-psychological subcortical processing. Thus, if the claim asserts that threat detection can literally occur without awareness of some target of threat, then this is problematic. Evaluating something as a threat is precisely that—an evaluation, and so threat detection cannot be reduced to non-psychological processing. The critical point to recognise here, though, is that even if a situation is evaluated as threatening, it does not necessarily follow that any such threat detection is *consciously* recognised, such that the person not only detects some target to be a threat *but is also aware* that a threat has been detected. As developed in Chapter 2, although a mental act involves a psychological relation of knowing, that knowing itself is not itself automatically known and instead requires a further mental act of reflection upon the first. As such, any threat-evaluation is itself necessarily unknown in the first instance. Instead, becoming aware of this evaluation would instead require a second mental act. This means that, for threat evaluation to occur, some target must be cognised and evaluated as a threat. However, this does not mean that the person is necessarily aware of that same evaluation. Consequently, if the claim here is simply that a person can evaluate x to be a threat (mediated by the functioning amygdala, for instance) and that this threat detection can occur unconsciously (such that S evaluates x to be a threat but is unaware of this evaluation), then this is a perfectly legitimate claim to make.

Appraisal, motivation, and affective responses

The discussion above implicates personality more broadly and raises questions as to what precisely stands as the knower in the threat-detecting relation. We presumably wish to avoid treating brain parts such as the amygdala as homunculi or censors that somehow engage in psychological activities and make decisions in the way that we would ordinarily attribute to persons. Nevertheless, threat appraisal implicates a larger view of personality, including a place for both motivational and affective states (Henry & Maze, 1989; Mackay, 1997). The topic of motivation and affective processes is, of course, complex, and here is not the place to review respective theories (see, however, Boag, 2017). Suffice it here to say that motivational states are taken here to be what *moves* or drives behaviour, both in sense of the causal factors underlying driven behaviour, as well as the determinants of the direction of those behaviours. Affects may stand as a further class of motivational states entailing particular ternary relations involving an experiencing subject S feeling x about some state of affairs y (see Boag, 2017). Both motivation and affects are directly relevant to understanding threat detection because these factors determine whether any event constitutes either a threat or not. That is, threat detection is linked to pre-existing motives and their affective responses.

Traumatisation and cognition

One implication from the above is that threat detection is not simply a cognitive exercise involving beliefs, as is sometimes taken to be the case. For example, "cognitive accounts" of traumatisation based on Kelly's Personal Construct theory (Kelly, 1955) propose that the manner in which events are construed impacts upon how the event is experienced. Loss of meaning plays an explanatory role in such account insofar as trauma results from an experience "that has occurred … outside the individual's usual construct system" (Sewell et al., 1996, p. 81). In plainer language, this can be taken to mean that certain experiences violate one's understanding of the world, and as a result, the new experiences remain dissociated because they cannot be accommodated into the established ways of understanding: "trauma produces isolated construct classes that cannot enter into transitive or associative relationships with the rest of the conceptual system" (Sewell et al., 1996, p. 81). Such a view, in and of itself, is not necessarily problematic. However, beliefs alone are not sufficient for explaining what any person does, since one and the same belief can be used to either promote or inhibit the same activity. For example, the belief that a certain diet might lead to weight loss might be acted upon if someone desires to lose weight, but not if someone desires the opposite (Maze, 1987). Instead, to explain why someone acts upon a belief requires addressing motivational states.[12] As Henry and Maze (1989) write: "Beliefs or constructs concerning matters of fact are made use of by *already existing* motives; beliefs do not generate motives or behavior independently of them" (p. 179, italics in original; cf. Mackay, 1997). Even in the case of so-called moral beliefs, which are taken to imply undertaking certain courses of action rather than others (i.e., it is good to tell the truth), motivation is nevertheless smuggled into a seemingly cognitive concept to explain why one person but not another will act upon the belief. Henry and Maze (1989), for example, postulate that fear of punishment provides the motive for acting in accordance with moral values:

> … moral beliefs, lacking actual referents, really conceal underlying motives, and, most especially, conceal fears of punishment, which are mediated by secondary anxieties such as fearing to lose the respect of significant others, and so on. From this viewpoint, it is these underlying fears that will be decisive for action, rather than the spurious cognitive content of the constructs "good" and "evil".
>
> (p. 180)

Whether Henry and Maze's thesis is correct here or not is an empirical question, but there is theoretical justification for proposing that motivational states determine whether any given situation is gratifying or frustrating and results in certain affective experiences (cf. Maze, 1973, 1987b). Thus, Mackay (2002) writes that the meaning attributed to events cannot be divorced from the mind's motives:

> Psychological meaning (meaningfulness) is motivational salience, that where some object, event, experience has particular salience to a person's interests— established, it is important to note, via the person's construing those objects consciously or unconsciously as means for effecting desires. Now, something does not have psychological meaning just because it stands for something else. Rather, it is meaningful in that it plays some special part in the person's motivational economy. It is because a person hates, fears, or desires something that it has psychological meaning (salience) for that person.
>
> (p. 7)

Consequently, any appraisal itself implicates a role for affects and motivational states, and it is simply not possible to reduce traumatisation to "shattered assumptions" as found in personal construct approaches or cognitive models of PTSD (e.g., Edmundson et al., 2011). Without addressing motivation, we are unable to determine the policy for affective responses or why loss of meaning impacts upon one person and not another. As such, although one's sense of meaning in life may be fundamentally altered during traumatisation, such meaning is not divorced from the motivational-affective foundations of the mind.

Of course, understanding the motivational-affective foundations of the mind involved in traumatisation requires a greater understanding of the person. As Wheaton and Montazer (2010) write, stressors are "conditions of threat, challenge, demands, or structural constraints that, by the very fact of their occurrence or existence, call into question the operating integrity of the organism" (p. 173). If so, making sense of traumatisation requires knowing what the "operating integrity of the organism" might be. One part of the problem here, however, is that it is not entirely clear how best to make sense of the functioning person. This makes it impossible then to objectively judge what constitutes a normal or pathological response (see Leising et al., 2009). Any answer to this question requires a theory of persons, along with the mechanisms and their role in the life of the organism.

On the other hand, although affective responses are consistently implicated in traumatisation (e.g., terror, guilt—Amstadter & Vernon, 2008), these need not be restricted to fear since emotions such as humiliation, anger, shame, and guilt may actually occur more frequently than anxiety in PTSD (see Pugh, Taylor & Berry, 2015). There may even be "moral injuries" that occur after deeply held moral values and beliefs are violated (where, for example, a soldier might be torn between stopping to help severely injured children or continuing driving to avoid being ambushed; see Farnsworth et al., 2014). McNally (2003b) here notes, that this possibility "underscores the moral complexity of trauma..." (p. 237), but even more than that, such findings indicate that traumatisation is a complex psychological state of affairs, potentially involving psychological conflict, a topic to be addressed in later chapters.

Summary

Although trauma is understood in various ways, the view that trauma causes dissociation as commonly stated is oversimplistic. Traumatisation is necessarily a complex relation involving the long-standing effects of events upon persons nested within broader (social) systems. Given that traumatisation is also necessarily a psychological process, any theory of traumatisation requires an account of threat-evaluation embedded within an account of the person. As such, a better approach then is to discuss the process of traumatisation and address the respective roles of cognition, motivation, and affects. However, to satisfactorily address this point, we need to consider what it means to be a "person" and the nature of mind. By way of first considering this, we turn to the two major explanatory directions of traumatisation and dissociation: Janetian accounts that explain trauma-dissociation in terms of a failure of integration, and psychodynamically oriented accounts, viewing dissociative symptoms in relation to defence against "overwhelming" affects resulting from traumatic situations.

Notes

1 However, it is also worth noting that an expanding range of symptom presentations has also been criticised. Galatzer Levy and Bryant (2013), for example, write that the diagnostic criteria have "become increasingly obscured as the diagnosis expands to encompass more heterogeneous presentations" (p. 651). By way of example, DSM-IV criteria permit 79,794 possible symptom combinations of PTSD, whereas DSM-5 increases this heterogeneity to 636,120 combinations (Galatzer Levy & Bryant, 2013).

2 Traumatisation is also associated with a broader variety of responses and symptoms than simply PTSD alone. As such, given the complexity of factors associated with traumatization, "[a] more general definition of trauma, uncoupled from the diagnosis of PTSD, therefore would be preferable" (Dalenberg et al., 2017, p. 22).

3 Thus, when McNally (2010) contends that "the more we broaden the concept of trauma, the less convincingly we can award causal significance to the stressor itself, and the

more we must emphasise vulnerability factors in the aetiology of PTSD" (p. 387), the problem is not located where he thinks it is. Contrary to McNally's view, addressing vulnerability factors is a step towards recognising causal complexity. McNally (2010), of course, accepts that risk factors are relevant to understanding PTSD but writes that if "risk factors overwhelmingly account for the emergence of PTSD in response to minor stressors" (p. 388), then this somehow diminishes the rationale of PTSD. PTSD is, of course, distinct from simply being upset by events, and we need to also avoid a situation where we "overmedicalise normal emotional responses" (p. 388). At the same time, what constitutes a "minor stressor" is open to interpretation, and many factors might impact upon what any individual experiences as either a major or minor stressor.

4 Freud (1919d) did, however, indicate that conflict might be present in "war neuroses", as a special class of traumatic neuroses.

5 Notwithstanding the fact that Freud's economic account of psychical energy is fatally flawed (see Boag, 2017).

6 The broader issue here concerns "capacity" explanations, whereby either resilience or being overwhelmed is explained in terms of the individual's "capacity" to adequately cope. Using "abilities" and "capacities" is a relatively common explanatory strategy in psychological science, where, for instance, someone's skill or behaviour is explained in terms of their "capacity" (see Howe, 1990). The problem here, however, is that terms such as "ability" and "capacity" easily invoke the problem of circular explanation since the terms are not logically independent of what they are intended to explain: "ability" basically means what one *is able to do*, and "capacity" means simply what one *is capable of*, and so basically provides a description of someone's performance (or likelihood of performing in a given way at any given time). See Boag (2011) for further discussion.

7 However, as will be developed in the following chapter, whether dissociation serves a defensive function is disputable, and there are difficulties with explaining how defensive dissociation might sensibly operate given issues of teleology. Moreover, accounts of defensive dissociation complicate matters further, by equating dissociation with the very coping mechanisms that are said to help the individual avoid becoming overwhelmed.

8 See also Tonhajzerova and Mestanik (2017), for discussion of physiological stress responses, as well as allostasis and anticipatory stress responses.

9 Given this, any affective state, such as where S fears x, also cannot be reduced to non-cognitive processes since judging something to be dangerous necessarily involves a psychological evaluation of a situation.

10 As a side note, DSM-5 re-classified PTSD as a "trauma- and stressor-related disorder" rather than as an anxiety disorder (APA, 2013), based on the observation that emotional reactions to the event (i.e., fear, helplessness, horror) do not appear necessary for PTSD to develop. However, this re-classification does not recognise the possibility of unconscious emotional responses that occur but are simply not reflected upon.

11 It should also be borne in mind, however, that the amygdala appears to be implicated in a variety of motivational, affective, and cognitive activities (see LeDoux & Schiller, 2009, pp. 52–53).

12 As discussed in Chapter 2, rather than striving towards goals, motivation needs to be instead conceptualised in terms of causal antecedents that push or drive the person into action and determine the direction of any such activity (Maze, 1983). As developed in Chapter 5, one way of addressing this is in terms of the motivational (action) systems that provide a basis for motivational policy.

Chapter 4

Foundations of modern theories of dissociation

The conceptual problem surrounding the claim that trauma causes dissociation necessitates a re-evaluation of the theoretical foundations of the two major approaches to dissociation found today. These foundations are traceable back to the works of Pierre Janet and Sigmund Freud, and although much has already been written over their respective contributions (e.g., Craparo, Ortu & Van der Hart, 2019; Ellenberger, 1970; Van der Hart & Dorahy, 2014), the explanatory value of these perspectives has not yet been assessed using the current conceptual framework. The two theories also differ in important respect: Janet is typically accredited with formulating a "passive-deficit" model of dissociation that explains trauma-dissociation in terms of a failure of integration. Freud, on the other hand, provides an "active-conflict" model, whereby later contributors view dissociation as a defence against "overwhelming" affects arising from traumatic situations (Dell, 2009; Gullestad, 2005; Lesley & Varvin, 2016). At the same time, Freud is seen eschewing dissociation in favour of "repression", whereas Janet is accredited with providing the basis for modern theories of trauma and dissociation (see Van der Hart & Horst, 1989; Van der Kolk, Herron & Hostetler, 1994). In fact, Van der Hart and Dorahy (2023) go so far as to write, that "[o]f the many theorists of dissociation, Pierre Janet … unquestionably presented the most detailed and articulate account of the connection between division in the personality/multiplication of personalities (i.e., dissociation) and hysteria" (p. 16).

The actual theoretical situation is, however, not so straightforward, and although the Janetian and Freudian-derived positions are generally considered distinct traditions (Kluft, 2000; MacIntosh, 2013; Whitmer, 2001), various authors believe that the distinction between dissociation and repression is actually not so clear cut (Cardeña, 1994; Dell, 2009). Dell (2009), for example, notes that in practice, dissociation and repression are typically conflated, to the extent that "our modern *de facto* understanding of dissociation is an undifferentiated tangle of Freudian repression and the Janetian subconscious" (p. 725). Such a tangle, of course, likely contributes to the conceptual confusion surrounding dissociation (cf. Cardeña & Gleaves, 2007. Furthermore, there are also a number of challenges with both the Janetian and Freudian positions for explaining how dissociation could occur and be maintained. Consequently, a fresh examination of the foundations of theories

DOI: 10.4324/9781003328254-4

of dissociation using a relational analysis is warranted, with specific focus on the explanatory factors of dissociation and their respective theories of mind.

The aim of this chapter is to assess Janet's and Freud's contributions and offer a preliminary critique of the foundations supporting contemporary theoretical perspectives on dissociation. This chapter will begin by discussing Janet's contribution to dissociation, before then contrasting his position with the Freudian-derived perspective. The nature of subconscious and unconscious processes will be further addressed, along with initial consideration of the possibility of multiple knowers existing within one and the same person. As will be shown, there are theoretical gaps and problems associated with both Janet's account of subconscious ideas and Freudian-derived explanations of defence. Furthermore, clarifying both the nature of subconscious and unconscious mental processes, along with the possibility of multiple knowers, is imperative for developing a coherent theory of personality dissociation.

Personality, consciousness, and the retraction of consciousness

Janet is taken to be "the first to recognize the connection between hysterical divisions/multiplications and exposure to traumatic stress" (Van der Hart & Dorahy, 2023, p. 28. His theory emerged within an intellectual *Zeitgeist* that encompassed the work of contributors such as Charcot, Möbius, Bernheim, Ribot, amongst others (see Van der Hart & Dorahy, 2014; Van der Hart & Friedman, 2019). Janet (1901) himself writes that it was Charcot at the Salpêtrière who was the first to scientifically study dissociation in the context of hysteria. Charcot contributed the view that traumatising events led to hysteria by antagonising a "congenital" predisposing weakness—a position informed at the time by the widely accepted theory of "degeneration" (Dell, 2009; Spiegel, 1986). Janet appears to have followed Charcot here, proposing that predisposing factors could interact with stress-inducing "accidental" environmental events to induce psychopathology (cf. Heim & Bühler, 2006, 2019). Janet (1901, 1907) notes, however, that many provoking factors—including intoxication, physical illness, and developmental periods such as puberty—could all be causally implicated. He writes:

Pathological heredity plays in hysteria, as in all other mental maladies, a rôle absolutely preponderant. A very great number of circumstances play the part of "provocative agents," and manifest by accidents this latent predisposition; they are hæmorrhages, wasting and chronic diseases, infectious diseases, typhoid fever in particular, and, in certain cases, the autointoxications, the organic diseases of the nervous system; various intoxications, physical or moral shocks, overwork, either physical or moral, painful emotions, and especially a succession of that sort of emotions the effects of which are cumulative, etc. It is easy to see that all these provocative agents are of the same character; they weaken the organism and increase the depression of the nervous system.

(p. 526)

What these factors had in common was that they could "exhaust" the nervous system, which manifested as a "retraction of consciousness". Such a retraction meant that the afflicted individual could only have "in their conscious thought a very limited number of facts" (Janet, 1901, p. 502):

> It is easy to see, in studying the absent-mindedness of hystericals, that their field of consciousness is very small; it is filled entirely with one relatively simple sensation, one remembrance, a small group of motor images, and cannot contain others at the same time. This limitation of the field of consciousness is but a manifestation of the general cerebral exhaustion which has been often admitted.
>
> (Janet, 1901, p. 502)

This retraction of consciousness could lead to pathology, however, since consciousness plays an important and specific role in personality formation. For Janet, the field of consciousness normally provides a synthetic character that facilitates the interconnection of various components of experience. Here, consciousness and personality appear to be coextensive, insofar personality extends only as far as the single stream of consciousness involved in integrating experience. He writes:

> We have proposed to call *"field of consciousness* or maximum extension of consciousness" the largest number of simple, or relatively simple, phenomena, which might be gathered at every moment, which might be simultaneously connected with our personality in one and the same personal perception".
>
> (Janet, 1901, p. 501, italics in original)

Janet thus believes that consciousness and the wholeness of personality are thus inextricably connected since personality entails the synthesis of these components into a "whole" experience. He writes, "this perception of a whole, ... is called personality" (Janet, 1901, p. 249), and such "personal perception" "consists essentially in synthesising these elementary facts and connecting them with the former notion of personality" (p. 259). Here Janet (1901) invokes an orchestral metaphor to illustrate his point: "A chief of orchestra, hearing simultaneously all the instruments, and following by reading or his memory the partition of the opera, unites in each of his states of consciousness an immense number of facts" (pp. 500–501). As such, the personality (as the chief of orchestra) appears to be the knowing subject or self whose ongoing role is to become conscious of mental content so as to more or less synthesise the various objects of cognition within the subject's experience. Janet refers to this subject term of cognition as the "principal personality" (Janet, 1901, p. 354), and Dell (2009) proposes that Janet used "personality" as "the conscious functioning of the ego or self" (p. 723). Dell's claim here is not unjustified given the general usage of the term "personality" around the turn of the 20th century (see Zachar & Krueger, 2013).[1]

Exhaustion and the impact upon personality

Exhaustion and the subsequent retraction of consciousness rendered the affected individual incapable of incorporating the various components of experience into a unified stream of consciousness. Consequently, this retraction prevented the assimilation of content into the principal personality. The specific mechanism here can be described as a deficit: the individual is in a state of mind where they are simply incapable of incorporating new material within a single stream consciousness. Janet (1901) writes:

> This exhaustion, we think, is described with more precision when we say: *It is a special moral weakness, consisting in the lack of power on the part of the feeble subject to gather, to consciousness psychological phenomena, and assimilate them to his personality.*
>
> (p. 502, italics in original)

As such, this "retraction" of consciousness appears to be more a failure of attention rather than an active withdrawal of consciousness (see Van der Hart & Friedman, 2019). Dell (2009) further writes that Janet's position might be described as a "deficient mode of what we would today call 'information-processing'" (Dell, 2009, p. 805). In other words, any material that is not initially encoded remains excluded from the rest of the personality thereafter.

Although such a failure of encoding might help clarify how aspects of experience are later irretrievable (because such experiences were never encoded in the first place), explaining how this specifically functions in the case of traumatisation requires greater consideration. As discussed in the previous chapter, traumatising events necessarily involve psychological appraisal and so there must be some initial registration of the threatening stimulus. This issue will be addressed later in Chapter 6. Suffice it here to say that dissociation is, in any event, an *effect* or symptom of exhaustion in Janet's account, rather than acting as a primary *cause* of psychopathology, even if secondary pathologies may follow (cf. Ortu & Craparo, 2019).

On the persistence of the unassimilated

Mental phenomena that are not personally synthesised do not simply disappear and instead persist as "fixed ideas" (*idées fixes*) (Janet, 1901, 1907a). These ideas exist *subconsciously* and lead to a deficit in experience: "[e]very subconscious idea robs the principal personality of sensations and images" (Janet, 1901, p. 354). Such fixed ideas could be produced artificially (e.g., via post-hypnotic suggestion) or could occur naturally via "accidental causes", as in the case of traumatising experiences:

> Fixed ideas are for us phenomena of this kind; that is to say, psychological phenomena which are developed in the mind in an automatic manner, outside the

will and the personal perception of the patient, but which, instead of being, like suggestions, experimentally called forth, are formed naturally under the influence of accidental causes. This difference in the artificial or natural provocation of automatic phenomena has, from a clinical and especially therapeutic point of view, quite grave consequences to justify this distinction. Ideas of this kind have been described at length in the case of patients considered as lunatics. They went under the name of obsessions, impulsions, phobias...

(Janet, 1901, p. 278)

In both cases, fixed ideas give rise to "automatic" responses that occur independently of the person's ordinary volition. Given that these ideas are unavailable to ordinary consciousness, these ideas cannot be resisted and inhibited. As Janet (1901) writes, "[t]his absence of resistance, of personal will in subconscious acts is explained in a very simple way: the subject is ignorant of them" (p. 258). Instead, for one thought to oppose another, they must "be united in the same consciousness" (Janet, 1907a, p. 274). Consequently, if an idea could enter the mind of an individual while bypassing the personal consciousness (via hypnosis or distraction), then the idea could develop unopposed by the rest of the personality.[2] The end effect, as Janet (1901) writes, is that "the subject has sustained a loss in his personality and that he is no longer master of his own thought" (p. 222).

Another consequence of subconscious ideas lying outside the control of the normal personality is that they could evolve into exaggerated forms. Janet (1901) here writes:

The exaggerated development of certain ideas depends on their isolation, and this isolation is a consequence of the retraction of the field of consciousness. The exaltation of the automatic phenomena springs generally from a diminution in the power of the voluntary activity which at every instant of our life reunites the present phenomena. It is the ensemble of these conceptions that we have designated by the name of *mental disintegration*.

(pp. 505–506, italics in original)

Of course, we have to ask why any such idea should increase in strength simply because it is unnoticed. Presumably any answer to this requires some consideration of the underlying motivational sources of the ideas. Nevertheless, suffice it here to say that these postulates (lack of control and exaggeration) provide Janet with an explanation for intrusive psychopathological hysterical phenomena: not only are fixed ideas uncontrollable, they also become stronger and intrude upon consciousness. Such intrusions are not, however, in any way integrated or assimilated into consciousness but instead appear alien to the normal personality. As Janet (1901) writes, "[v]ery often the patients complain of an idea, an image, which suddenly invades their mind without their knowing why" (Janet, 1901, p. 265). This raises, however, a further question as to why such ideas remain uncontrollable when seemingly available to consciousness.

Fixed ideas and the division of personality

A part-answer to this question above lies in Janet's view that fixed ideas are not simply units of information but are instead manifestations of the active "functions" of personality. What these functions specifically consist of is not entirely clear, but they do include the "organic wants and ... the acts that are connected with them" (Janet, 1907a, p. 319). This being so, fixed ideas then encompass ideational, motivational, and behavioural "functional units" that no longer serve a role in the principal personality:

> What is dissolved is personality, the system of grouping of the different functions around the same personality. I maintain to this day that, if hysteria is a mental malady, it is not a mental malady like any other, impairing the social sentiments or destroying the constitution of ideas. It is a malady of the *personal synthesis... Hysteria is a form of mental depression characterized by the retraction of the field of personal consciousness and a tendency to the dissociation and emancipation of the systems of ideas and functions that constitute personality.*
>
> (Janet, 1907a, p. 332, italics in original)

In connection to traumatisation, "[t]he dissociation bears on the function that was in full activity at the moment of a great emotion" (Janet, 1907a, p. 33), which, as a separate function, results in "*a complete and permanent division of the personality, to the formation of several groups independent of each other*" (Janet, 1901, p. 527, italics in original). Relatively transient cases of undoubling of consciousness could be evident in various phenomena including post-hypnotic suggestion and intoxication. With hysteria, however, the undoubling is both more permanent and absolute. Janet (1901) writes: "In hysteria the psychological phenomena, not being of a nature to be fully reunited, clearly separate into several groups in a way independent of each other" (p. 523). Since the source of fixed ideas is independent of the functions in the principal personality, such ideas might be known but act nevertheless autonomously. Mental content associated with fixed ideas might then be able to intrude upon the principal personality without being amenable to correction and inhibition.

As a result, these independent groups reflect an "undoubling of the personality" (Janet, 1901, p. 453): "*Hysteria is a form of mental disintegration characterised by a tendency toward the permanent and complete undoubling (dédoublement) of the personality*" (Janet, 1901, p. 528, italics in original).[3] That is, we have two independent streams of consciousness typically manifesting as two alternating personality states. These were described variously as a "double character" (Janet, 1907a, p. 69), a "normal" and "abnormal existence" (p. 74), "two alternating periods" (p. 74), "different psychological states" (p. 83), or "different existences" (p. 84). These states might differ from one another in character, intellectual functioning, and memory and could manifest as either discrete or overlapping experiences, such that the individual may vacillate between an "ordinary" personality state and the dissociated one, or have both present simultaneously (Janet, 1907a).

Either way, Janet believes that these are *parallel* streams of consciousness (as opposed to simply alternating ones) since even if one of these states is dominant to the apparent exclusion of the other, the other nevertheless co-exists (Janet, 1907a, 1907b). At the same time, Janet did not believe that the dissociation between the parts was typically absolute, writing that the "absolute division of life into two alternating periods which do not know each other at all is quite exceptional: we can connect only a small number of cases" (Janet, 1907a, p. 74; cf. Janet, 1901, p. 493).

On the subconscious and multiple knowers

Based on the discussion above, the manifestation of fixed ideas cannot be stopped by the principal personality, not simply because the mental content is "not known" (since the content can clearly be taken as the object of cognition), but rather because there are different sources of the mental content constituting different *knowers*. In this respect, the cognitive activity of a dissociated personality is not directly amenable to correction by the principal personality, in the same way, that one person cannot directly control the thoughts of another. Janet thus appears to clearly endorse the possibility of multiple knowers existing within one and the same person. He notes that although subconscious acts arise independently from the principal personality, such acts must nevertheless involve a type of "intelligence", and so must involve a rudimentary form of consciousness (i.e., such acts cannot be reduced to non-psychological reflex-like responses) (Janet (1907a, 1907b). For this reason, Janet appears to object to employing the term "unconscious" to describe the state of the split-off ideas since if the term is taken to mean something stripped of any consciousness, then it is not fit for describing the split-off parts of the personality. He proposes instead that "subconscious" is the preferred term to reflect that some degree of consciousness must nevertheless be involved:

> A bit of attention suffices to let us notice certain actions that we, without knowing them, carried out when we were distracted. Little perceptions exist in sleep and also in complicated dreams, for which we are scarcely able to account ourselves. Such phenomena were called unconscious, i.e. existing without any consciousness. This description is only correct if one takes the term 'consciousness' in an absolute sense and if one uses it to denote the clearest consciousness of personality ('l'idée de personnalité'). But it seems more correct for us to call them subconscious phenomena in which the elementary consciousness exists but not an explicit consciousness of the personality".
>
> (Janet in and translated by Bühler & Heim, 2009, p. 191)

Commenting on this, Bühler and Heim (2009) write, "according to Janet, a subconscious psychological act has all the features of a conscious act, except that it is not known by the particular person at the moment at which it is carried out" (p. 194). If this is the case, then there is merit to Janet's position here, since there is no logical objection to proposing that there are acts that involve knowing or "intelligence" but are themselves unknown. However, there are two senses of consciousness being employed here, and Janet's point can also be taken to mean that the acts are not simply unknown to the individual, but that there is at least a second elementary stream of consciousness (a second knower), independent of the "clearest consciousness of the personality" (the principal personality). For example, Janet (1901) notes that subconscious acts are nonetheless conscious but differ from ordinary ones with respect to being independent from the principal personality:

> this phenomenon is not conscious in the same way as the voluntary act is; we do not in this instance say: "I, me, Mr. So-and-so, I make the motion of walking, eating, writing. It calls forth only isolated phenomena of consciousness, and does not come within this perception of a whole, which is called personality.
>
> (p. 249)

Ortu and Craparo (2019) accordingly write, "[r]ather than an absence of consciousness, we should speak here of a division of consciousness" (p. 30), whereby multiple streams of consciousness exist.

If this interpretation is correct, then there are broader questions concerning the nature of personality generally. Is there, for instance, a single knower or stream of consciousness to begin with, that then subsequently becomes divided? Or are there multiple knowers to begin with initially, with the task of personality to unite these into a single stream of consciousness? For his part, Janet (1907b) does not rule out the possibility of mental plurality existing in non-pathological cases—he leaves it as an empirical question—but he does ordinarily treat it as a pathological occurrence (a "disease of the personality"; p. 65). In this latter respect, Janet's account here is taken to provide the basis for the claim that traumatisation *leads to* divisions of personality (Van der Hart et al., 2006; Van der Hart & Freidman, 2019). Van der Hart and Dorahy (2023), for example, write that Janet believed that "vehement or violent emotions lead to the division of the personality into dissociative 'systems of ideas and functions,' ... that had their own phenomenal awareness" (p. 17). In turn, these parts "develop higher psychological functions, such as autonomous will and critical judgement" (Van der Hart & Friedman, 2019, p. 11), along with "their own identities, life histories, and enduring patterns of perceiving, thinking about, and relating to the environment" (p. 12).

There are, however, questions concerning even the possibility of multiple knowers, and Dell (2009) argues here, that in this respect, Janet "did not theorize about the causes of mental disaggregation so much as he offered descriptive generalizations (of the phenomena that he has repeatedly observed)" (p. 722). Janet (1907b), for his part, does, in fact, say that his reference to the subconscious "is not a philosophical explanation" but rather "a simple clinical observation" (p. 65). On the other hand, Dell (2009) argues that any retraction of the field of consciousness could not qualify as the cause of personality splitting since it is an alteration of consciousness rather than the formation of a second mind. Thus, one potential gap in Janet's theory concerns accounting for how multiple streams of consciousness (i.e., multiple knowers) arise. As will be shown in Chapter 5, there is merit to this criticism, but the possibility of multiple knowers is nevertheless defencible.

Dissociation and dynamic defence

Janet's contemporaries, Joseph Breuer and Sigmund Freud, also postulated a splitting of consciousness resulting from trauma, and initially provided two possible avenues for this to occur (Breuer & Freud, 1895). Breuer's favoured explanation was in terms of "hypnoid states", consisting of "abnormal" dream-like states of consciousness in which "the ideas which emerge in them are very intense but are cut off from associative communication with the rest of the content of consciousness" (Breuer in Breuer & Freud, 1895d, p. 12). If a traumatising experience occurred during such states, then the memory of the event would fail to become integrated into the mainstream of consciousness and would instead remain in an isolated yet pathological condition. This essentially Janetian-passive account could be contrasted with a second active, dynamic account of "repression". This involved "a question of things which the patient wished to forget, and therefore intentionally repressed from his conscious thought and inhibited and suppressed" (Breuer & Freud, 1895d, p. 10). This motivated "fending off" of painful or shameful memories prevented such mental content from further association with conscious thinking (Freud in Breuer & Freud, 1895d, p. 157). Although Freud appears to have initially accepted Breuer's hypnoid state basis for hysteria, he nevertheless came to prioritise repression (or more broadly defence[4]), even expressing doubts concerning the existence of hypnoid states:

> Strangely enough, I have never in my own experience met with a genuine hypnoid hysteria. Any that I took in hand has turned into a defence hysteria [and] … I am unable to suppress a suspicion that somewhere or other the roots of hypnoid and defence hysteria come together, and that the primary factor is defence.

> (Freud in Breuer & Freud, 1895d, p. 286)

Freud went on to initially explain adult psychopathology in terms of repressed memories of actual child sexual abuse (what came to be known as the "seduction hypothesis"), but soon recanted this theory, instead believing that the reports of seduction were actually imaginative falsifications or "screen memories" (Freud, 1899).[5] The targets of repression were instead what can be broadly thought of as "desires" (wishful impulses and their associated fantasies), and with this emerges psychoanalysis proper: some forms of psychopathology—first referred to as "defence neuroses" and then later as "psychoneuroses"—resulted from *psychical conflict*, "a struggle between motive forces of different degrees of strength or intensity" (Freud in Breuer & Freud, 1895d, p. 270). In contrast to Janet's position, Freud believed that his approach

> had the merit of entering into the interplay of the psychical forces and of thus bringing the mental processes in hysteria nearer to normal ones, instead of characterising the neurosis as nothing more than a mysterious disorder insusceptible to further analysis.
>
> (Freud, 1906a, p. 276)

Additionally, Freud on numerous occasions took particular issue with Janet's conclusion that hysteria was primarily due to "congenital degeneracy" (e.g., Freud, 1894a, p. 46; 1913m, p. 207), arguing instead that any such exhaustion or weak-mindedness was, if anything, the result of repression (see Eagle, 2000a for extensive discussion). Summing up the differences between his theory and Janet's, Freud writes:

> You will now see in what the differences lies between our view and Janet's. We do not derive the psychical splitting from an innate incapacity for synthesis on the part of the mental apparatus, we explain it dynamically, from the conflict of opposing mental forces and recognize it as the outcome of an active struggling on the part of the two psychical groupings against one another.
>
> (Freud, 1910a, pp. 25–26)

Despite the apparent differences between Freud's and Janet's approaches, the *outcome* of repression is broadly the same as that of dissociation—there is a certain splitting of consciousness (cf. Erdelyi, 1990; Tarnopolsky, 2003). Furthermore, as Hart (1910) recognises, "[t]he phenomenon of dissociation has not been disputed by Freud—on the contrary, it takes a prominent place amongst the circumstances which he desires to explain" (p. 369). As such, the main distinction between Janet and Freud thus concerns the respective accounts of the mechanism of dissociative pathology, *viz.* whether the mind is incapable of integration (Janet) or actively resists it (Freud), a distinction described variously as deficit versus defence, or passive disaggregation versus active splitting (Dell, 2009; Gullestad, 2005; Van der Kolk et al., 1994).

Challenges associated with Freud's theory of repression

In Janet's deficit model, subconscious ideas never enter the mainstream of consciousness in the first place and so simply fail to get assimilated. Freud, however, is necessarily committed to the viewpoint that the repressed target is known on at least one occasion and then actively rejected (see Boag, 2012, 2017). He writes, "*the essence of repression lies simply in turning something away, and keeping it at a distance, from the conscious*" (Freud, 1915d, p. 147, italics in original) and therein lies a theoretical difficulty with explaining how repression occurs.

With repression, the wishful impulses are not thereafter destroyed but instead persist and remain causally active given their endogenous sources (Freud, 1900a, 1915d). Freud here writes:

> The process of repression is not to be regarded as an event which takes place *once*, the results of which are permanent, as when some living thing has been killed and from that time onward is dead; repression demands a persistent expenditure of force, and if this were to cease the success of the repression would be jeopardized, so that a fresh act of repression would be necessary. We may suppose that the repressed exercises a continuous pressure in the direction of the conscious, so that this pressure must be balanced by an unceasing counter-pressure.
>
> (Freud, 1915d, p. 151, italics in original)

Freud thus needs to explain how the repressed is constantly prevented from becoming known in consciousness. This situation is further complicated, however, since the repressed target further acquires substitute aims in the form of phantasies (Freud, 1907a), which then attempt to force their way into both waking consciousness and dreams. These derivatives require further acts of repression, and so repression subsequently involves a two-stage operation, whereby the objectionable impulse is initially prevented from entering consciousness ("primal repression"), and the substitutive phantasies are thereafter targeted by "repression proper" (*eigentliche Verdrängung*) or "after-pressure" (*Nachdrängen*) (Freud, 1915d).

This dynamic picture allows Freud to explain the symptoms of the psycho-neuroses and other phenomena, such as dreams and slips, in terms of repressed wishes acquiring substitutive sources of gratification (e.g., Freud, 1926f, 1939a).[6] However, the specific problem here is explaining how an individual somehow actively ignores the content of their own mind (Boag, 2012; Maze & Henry, 1996), especially since Freud, from start to finish, proposes that the "ego"—the knowing, "conscious" part of the personality—is responsible for repression (Freud in Breuer & Freud, 1895, pp. 269, 278; Freud, 1940a, pp. 179–180). The specific theoretical difficulty here is this: since the "ego" is said to be both the repressing agency and the "victim" of repression, then the ego must somehow continuously guard against intrusions of the repressed. As Maze (1983), however, notes, the problem then is "explaining how the ego contrives not to know something when the contriving requires that it does know it" (p. 149).

Although this apparent paradox is not necessarily fatal to the Freudian account (see Boag, 2012), there is a problem with proposing that some type of censor or censors guard the ego from knowledge of the repressed. Freud, for instance, does attempt to metaphorically explain repression by reference to a "watchman" who prevents wishes in the unconscious system from entering consciousness: "on the threshold between these two rooms a watchman performs his function: he examines the different mental impulses, acts as a censor, and will not admit them into the drawing room if they displease him" (Freud, 1916–1917, p. 295). If this were to be the case, then Gardner (1993) correctly concludes that such a censoring agency must accordingly be some type of transcendental agency, superior to the ego, and capable of manipulating and even distorting mental content to deceive the conscious system. At the same time, since the only evidence for such a censor is the apparent censoring itself, then any such agency appears simply to be an instance of reification, whereby the supposed self-deceiving activity is reified into an agency performing that very same activity (see Boag, 2012, 2017, 2022 for further discussion).

A related potential problem with explaining repression involves teleology, whereby the defensive activity occurs *in order to* prevent negative affect from occurring in the first place. Zepf (2001), for example, unambiguously embraces teleology in his reading of Freud—"Freud considers the engine of mental life to be not an efficient but a final cause" (p. 469)—and so proposes that "the basis of the repression is seen to be not causal but a matter of intentionality" (p. 468). On this particular view, rather than repression being instigated by anxiety and distress acting as efficient causes, repression occurs *in order to* avoid unpleasure from occurring. This, however, raises a major explanatory problem. If repression occurs in order to avoid unpleasure rather than being triggered by distress, then the person must somehow be able to predict that some occurrence *x* is likely to result in unpleasure, to thereby instigate repression. This is, of course, a problem, since being able to predict that some occurrence *x* will incur unpleasure would require knowing what is to be repressed in the first place. As such, we would need to know the repressed in order to intentionally repress it (Boag, 2022).

Dissociation as defence

The discussion above highlights potential theoretical challenges in accounts postulating that dissociation serves a defensive function, and as will be shown, there are several problematic issues associated with repression that pertain also to defensive dissociation. Repression and dissociation are sometimes distinguished in terms of dissociative "vertical" splits and repressive "horizontal" splits, the former reflecting compartmentalisation of distressing content, rather than the content remaining in an unconscious state (e.g., Diseth, 2005; Eagle, 2001a; Ross, 2022; Stern, 2009). Kohut (1971), for example, proposes that incompatible personality states can exist side by side but isolated from one another (e.g., a reality-oriented self-view that remains isolated from a more infantile and grandiose self-view). Such distinctions between repression and dissociation can be difficult to strictly maintain, however (see Erdelyi, 1990), and others see terms such as repression and defence as essentially the same. Tarnopolsky (2003), for example, sees the terms as synonymous: "a trauma therapist is using the word 'dissociation,' where a British analyst would say 'splitting' and a classical Freudian would say 'repression'" (p. 11).

Whether these terms are, in fact, synonyms, is not easy to judge given various theoretical commitments held by the different positions. However, Dell (2009) writes that the common clinical usage of dissociation as a verb (where *S* dissociates) lends itself especially to a dynamic defensive view of dissociation since it implies that an individual *actively* engages in dissociation:

> whenever we use *dissociation* as a verb (especially as a transitive verb…), we are viewing dissociation through the lens of repression. When we do that, we are describing dissociation as an active, motivated, self-protective course of action. We are describing dissociation as a defense.
>
> (Dell, 2009, p. 722, italics in original)

Defensive dissociation is most commonly viewed as a protective response that minimises negative affective states associated with overwhelming and intensely stressful traumatising situations. Dell (2009), for instance, believes that dissociation takes on a protective role, since it "allows some people to split off awareness of uncomfortable memories and experiences" (p. 462). Bailey and Brand (2017) also write that "dissociation provides protection against emotional distress" (p. 170), and Şar (2014) similarly states that "[d]issociative disorders can be conceptualized as a syndrome oriented at self-protection in response to threat, in contrast to self-regulation which is the primary modus of functioning in a safe environment" (p. 173). Defensive dissociation here serves a protective function insofar as it "allows individuals to temporarily protect the mind from experiences that overwhelm their capacity for cognitive processing through a passive disengagement from reality and a compartmentalization of behaviors, thoughts, memories, and feelings related to trauma" (Schimmenti, 2018, pp. 553–554). As a protective function, defensive dissociation is also seen as a specific in-built type of mechanism for dealing with traumatisation (Howell & Itzkowitz, 2016a). Gullestad (2005), for instance, writes:

> It is generally agreed that dissociation resulting from traumatic experiences appears to be particularly prominent because it offers a psychological defence against overwhelming stimuli. In this perspective, dissociation is conceptualised as a basic part of the psychobiology of the human trauma response, implying a protective activation of altered states of consciousness in reaction to overwhelming psychological trauma.
>
> (pp. 640–641)

As an in-built protective mechanism, dissociation is believed to help prevent personality system failure, such that, "[i]n the face of imminent de-personalization and collapse of selfhood, the mind falls back on its ultimate safety measure" (Bromberg, 2003, p. 567). Thus, in contrast to Janet's approach, dissociation is not simply a passive failure but rather serves a specific purpose as an in-built protective mechanism.

By extension, the development of dissociative parts in DID is also seen as a defensive, adaptive response to traumatisation. On this view, the different identity states help keep various overwhelming experiences compartmentalised (e.g., Dalenberg et al., 2012; Dorahy et al., 2014). Dell and Eisenhower (1990), for example, write that DID (or as it, then was, MPD) is an "adaptive, dissociative response of a young child's mind to the fear and pain of overwhelming trauma—most commonly abuse" (p. 359). Middleton (2014) similarly comments that "[t]he genesis of dissociative identity disorder (DID) lies with chronic inescapable trauma in childhood, in that to avoid being overwhelmed or to minimize the affective response to traumas... the child dissociates" (p. 47). Critics similarly understand DID as serving a protective function, with Lynn et al. (2014) writing within the context of the "trauma-dissociation hypothesis", "people actually house multiple 'personalities' (i.e., alters) or poorly defined 'personality states'—which are somehow walled off or dissociated from everyday consciousness—to defend against thoughts and feelings stemming from traumatic experiences" (p. 897). Dissociation and DID thus are both commonly seen as responses serving a defensive purpose.

Alternatives to active defensive dissociation

Although defensive dissociation may serve a protective function, not all theorists propose that this defence is necessarily active. Stern (2009), for instance, attributes to Janet the view that

> dissociation represents the mind's fallback operation, a desperation move that takes place automatically when all else fails, a nonvolitional shutdown that protects the mind from coming apart. In this usage, which is no doubt still the most widespread, dissociation is not employed actively, as an unconscious defensive operation. It happens to people; they suffer it passively.
>
> (p. 84)

Whether this view can be attributed to Janet or not is debatable, but there is at least one hint in Janet's writing that dissociation might serve a passive defensive function by interacting with a vulnerability factor. Janet (1907a) here writes that

> [w]ith hystericals, in consequence of particular dispositions, the lowering of the nervous strength produces, in some manner, a superficial retraction; there is, as it were, an autotomy. Consciousness, which is no longer able to perform too complex operations, gives up some of them.
>
> (p. 334; cf. Janet, 1901, p. 523)

Janet's comparison here with "autotomy" is noteworthy with respect to what might be considered non-motivated defence, since the term presumably takes on the meaning introduced by the Belgian zoologist, Léon Fredericq, during the 1880s (see Wilkie et al., 2007). Here, autotomy is a zoological term referring to the biological phenomenon, whereby certain animals detach body parts such as tails or limbs for defensive purposes. For instance, a lizard might shed its tail once caught by a bird, whereby sacrificing the appendage allows the lizard to potentially avoid predation. In such cases, there is a preformed "breakage point", such that "autotomy always occurs at an anatomically distinct breakage plane at which there are specific adaptations for facilitating detachment, minimising tissue damage (via localised planes of weakness), minimising loss of body fluids, accelerating wound healing or promoting regeneration" (Wilkie et al., 2007, p. 286).[7] The analogy then is clear in the case of hysteria, whereby a pre-existing "weak spot" could provide a defensive breaking point, even if also becoming the focal point of psychopathology.

Of course, on the other hand, not everyone agrees that dissociation serves a defensive role, and Nijenhuis (2012) here disputes the defensive role of dissociation writing that although "[m]any authors regard dissociation as a mental defense, ... there is nothing defensive about positive dissociative symptoms" (p. 139). The reasoning here seems to be that since dissociative outcomes such as hearing voices or re-experiencing dissociative symptoms are associated with distress, such manifestations contradict the claim that dissociation serves a self-protective function. However, one consideration here is that the positive symptoms may be unintended or accidental consequences of a nevertheless defensive act. By way of analogy, a person driving a car who defensively avoids an approaching hazard may nevertheless be killed, not as an intended outcome, but as an unintended consequence of the defensive driving. Defensive dissociation could conceivably initially thus succeed in blunting the impact of some overwhelming event, but then also nevertheless act as a cause of undesired consequences such as the personality becoming pathologically divided. Freud similarly noted that such outcomes could similarly occur with repression:

> [defensive acts] do not always have the desired result, but lead to the formation of dangerous substitutes for the repressed and to burdensome reactions on the part of the ego. From these two classes of phenomena taken together there emerge what we call the symptoms of neuroses.
>
> (Freud, 1910i, p. 215)

Explaining defensive dissociation and the problem of teleology

There are, however, legitimate grounds for questioning the purposive defensive role of dissociation. One of these issues concerns the aforementioned teleology, and as with Zepf (2001) earlier, various psychodynamic authors appear relatively explicit about teleology in their accounts of dissociation. For example, teleology is apparent in Blizard's (2003) claim that "the child dissociates conflicting states in order to segregate experiences of caretaker nurturance from those of abuse" (p. 36). Teleology is further evident in Howell and Itzkowitz's (2016a) claim that the "very purpose" of dissociation is "to keep the person living in a world of partial truths, confusion caused by gaps in experience, and shifting dissociated self-states" (p. 16). These authors continue:

> Dissociative processes function to prevent the person from knowing the past, i.e., to obstruct knowledge of the past and to prevent it from breaking into consciousness and threatening to overwhelm the damaged, fragmented self and its tenuous hold on reality.
>
> (p. 16)

Purcell (2019), however, makes the fair point that "a mind reflexively dissociating can be easily mistaken for a mind intentionally defending itself" (p. 319), and as developed in Chapter 2, teleological claims may sometimes be simply shorthand for efficient causal explanations. In such cases, teleology is potentially harmless if such explanations can be re-worded non-teleologically. For example, if "purpose" in the above accounts simply refers to "shaped by natural selection" (cf. Dell, 2009), then there need not necessarily be a tension with efficient causality. Nevertheless, there are various logical problems with statements concerning dissociation as an adaptive response. Consider, for instance, Schimmenti and Caretti's (2016) claim that

> as a defense mechanism, dissociation represents an *adaptive* rather than maladaptive functioning of the mind, a basic process that enhances the integrating functions of the self by screening out excessive or irrelevant stimuli, thus allowing specific self-states to function optimally when full immersion in a single reality is exactly what is called or wished for.
>
> (p. 110, italics in original)

The potentially problematic element here is that "screening out" is presumably a psychological activity involving some form of judgement (e.g., assessing for potential danger through anticipating dangerous consequences). If this were to be the case, then any such scrutiny would require some kind of cognising agency to screen mental content and so act like the Freudian censor. A similar issue arises in connection to Bromberg's (2003) claim that defensive dissociative acts as an "early warning system". On Bromberg's view, dissociation is a process that helps prevent the recurrence of trauma:

> ... dissociation ... can become enlisted as a defense against trauma by disconnecting the mind from its capacity to perceive what is too much for selfhood and sometimes sanity to bear. It reduces what is in front of someone's eyes to a narrow band of perceptual reality ("whatever is going on is not happening to *me*"). As a defense against the *recurrence* of trauma, it creates a mental structure that serves as an "early warning system." Its key quality is its ability to retain the adaptational protection afforded by the hypnoid separateness of incompatible self-states.
>
> (p. 561, italics in original)

How any such dissociation could "create a mental structure that serves as an 'early warning system'" is not entirely clear, but if dissociation somehow acts against the recurrence of trauma, then this implies that the mind somehow foreshadows a catastrophic effect upon the self. If this is not the ego or general personality, then this would require some type of problematic cognising protective agency acting as censor.

There is, of course, no logical difficulty with postulating various in-built protective mechanisms that help maintain survival (e.g., the immune system), and it is possible to view dissociation as playing a non-teleological defensive role. One example of a non-teleological account of dissociative defence has recently been proposed by Purcell (2019) who views dissociation as "a protective *reaction* that occurs *reflexively* in traumatic experience" (p. 318, italics in original). Purcell compares dissociation here to a fight or flight response, something, then, which is an active response to perceived threat (e.g., fleeing in the face of a predator), but not something occurring in order to prevent threat from occurring in the first place. In this respect, Purcell (2019) writes that "dissociation in response to trauma is *entirely automatic*-purposeful but *not* intentional, consciously or unconsciously" (p. 318, italics in original), which can be taken to mean that threat perception triggers a defensive response without reflection and deliberation upon the act. By way of an example, an event might instigate vehement emotional responses such as overwhelming terror, which, in turn trigger defensive dissociative responses. This account is consistent with efficient causality since the defensive response occurs as an automatic reaction to painful stimuli rather than as purposive, intentional action[8] (i.e., without any "rational" decision by some agency to dissociate in order to prevent threat from being perceived in the first place). Of course, the source of threat is necessarily perceived or imagined in such an account (defence would not occur otherwise), but as developed in the previous chapter, there is no logical problem with proposing that defensive dissociation occurs unconsciously. In a similar vein, Gullestad (2005) proposes that "[t]he ego unconsciously perceives and 'knows' an approaching danger and initiates defensive activity" (p. 652), which might be taken to mean that the ego knows some threat x without knowing that x is known. Of course, what this "ego" precisely is requires consideration, and an explanation is also nevertheless still required for explaining how this defensive act occurs without self it becoming known (see Boag, 2012). As such, taken together, there are numerous challenges that any account of defensive dissociation must address, but as will be developed in Chapter 6, there is merit to the proposal that dissociation occurs as a non-purposive result of defensive activity.

A comment on the subconscious, unconscious, and the possibility of multiple knowers

One other area that requires further clarification concerns the precise relationship between subconscious and unconscious processes, in Janet's and Freud's account, respectively. To address this, it is worth drawing attention first to the various theoretical similarities between Janet's theory of dissociation and Freud's theory of repression. Despite their differences, in both accounts, there is some type of withdrawal or pulling back of attention of some event (i.e., retraction of consciousness; repression), resulting in a restricted awareness. Moreover, both accounts postulate that once attention is withdrawn, the content nevertheless persists, which is relevant to understanding certain forms of psychopathology. Both accounts similarly propose that since the content is isolated from the mainstream of consciousness, it is subsequently less susceptible to interference from other parts of the personality because the content is no longer available to conscious inspection. As seen earlier, Janet (1901) writes, "[t]he exaggerated development of certain ideas depends on their isolation, and this isolation is a consequence of the retraction of the field of consciousness" (p. 504).

Be that as it may, there are, of course, also noteworthy differences, in terms of the specific mechanisms (deficit/defence). Furthermore, with Janet, dissociation is the effect, whereas in a defensive sense, defensive dissociation acts as a cause of dissociative symptomatology. Additionally, the possibility of multiple knowers also requiring further comment. In this respect, Freud (1915e) was critical of the term "subconscious" and sceptical concerning the possibility of multiple knowers given the implication of a "consciousness below consciousness". Instead, for Freud, only a single knower or "consciousness" exists within the person, rather than multiple streams of consciousness within the one person. He writes:

We have no right to extend the meaning of this word [conscious] so far as to make it include a consciousness of which its owner himself is not aware. If philosophers find difficulty in accepting the existence of unconscious ideas, the existence of an unconscious consciousness seems to me even more objectionable.
(Freud, 1912g, p. 263; cf. 1915e, p. 170)

From Freud's perspective, the multiple streams of consciousness apparent in DID are explicable with respect to a single knower turning attention to different objects:

We shall also be right in rejecting the term 'subconsciousness' as incorrect and misleading. The well-known cases of '*double conscience*' (splitting of consciousness) prove nothing against our view. We may most aptly describe them as cases of a splitting of the mental activities into two groups, and say that the same consciousness turns to one or the other of these groups alternately.
(Freud, 1915e, pp. 170–171, italics in original)

Here, according to Freud, the ego is the single knowing agency, and it "is to this ego that consciousness is attached; the ego controls the approaches to motility… it is the mental agency which supervises all its own constituent processes" (Freud, 1923b, p. 17). However, although Freud is explicitly committed to the ego as a single knower, Cassullo (2019) rightly observes that Freud is, in fact, theoretically committed to postulating multiple knowers given the proposed interactions between various 'agencies' (see also Boag, 2014, 2017). This point has not been lost on others (e.g., Sartre, 1956), and was explicitly developed in various later psychodynamic perspectives embracing multiple knowers in object relational theories (most notably in Fairbairn's work (Fairbairn, 1952), and subsequently developed by Ogden (1993, 2002, 2010)). Whether postulating multiple knowers is logically viable or not is an issue critical for making sense of personality in DID, and as will be developed in the next chapter, whether such accounts can be coherently formulated requires further consideration.

Freud, of course, also championed the view that we are not necessarily aware of all the mind's contents (i.e., there are "unconscious mental processes"), and in this context, he writes critically concerning the meaning of the term "subconscious": "If someone talks of subconsciousness, I cannot tell whether he means the term topographically—to indicate something lying in the mind beneath consciousness—or qualitatively—to indicate another consciousness, a subterranean one, as it were" (Freud, 1926e, p. 198). Freud subsequently writes that "[t]he only trustworthy antithesis is between conscious and unconscious" (p. 198). Nevertheless, the theoretical situation here is not so clear cut and there is ample room for confusion given Freud's overlapping descriptive, dynamic, and systematic uses of the term "unconscious" (see Boag, 2017). The least problematic use of these is the "descriptive" (or epistemic) usage, whereby the term "unconscious" simply describes whatever is presently unknown (i.e., what is presently not attended to can be described as unconscious). Most of our beliefs, etc., while not the focus of our attention can be described as unconscious beliefs, etc., even if we can further attend to these mental content to make them the object of awareness (i.e., such that they become "conscious"). As seen earlier, the theoretical situation becomes more challenging, however, with the "dynamic" usage of the term, whereby some mental contents are forced out of awareness and then prevented from reaching conscious awareness (i.e., content becomes descriptively unconscious due to repression and then prevented from becoming conscious). The "systemic" sense complicates matters further, whereby the term "unconscious" refers to a specific mental system (the system *Ucs.*), sitting alongside the preconscious system (*Pcs.*), and conscious one (*Cs.*), each of which were theorised to operate in distinct and specific ways.

Suffice it here to say that Freud's systemic account has been variously criticised and can be rejected. This is because the systematic distinctions cannot be coherently maintained and so the justification for distinct systems is lacking (see Boag, 2012, 2017). One related issue here, however, concerns the implied spatial metaphor when postulating a (sub)consciousness *beneath* consciousness. Although it might be tempting to differentiate between "levels of consciousness" (e.g., Van der Hart & Friedman, 2019), one potential problem here is that such spatial metaphors easily lend themselves to locating mentality in a specific place, rather than appreciating the relational of nature of cognition. Aside from where such space might feasibly exist, postulating levels of consciousness also fails to address what is doing the knowing, the nature of the knowing relation, and what is in fact known. On a relational analysis, we instead need to clarify the distinction between consciousness as a knower and consciousness as a relationship between a knower and the known. Terms such as "personal consciousness" would suggest the former cf. (Ortu & Craparo, 2019, p. 31), whereas terms such as "altered states" or "alterations of consciousness" suggest the latter.

Janet, on the other hand, objects to employing the term "unconscious" to describe the state of split-off ideas, since, as he notes, acts that occur outside of awareness still necessarily require "intelligence" and so cannot be reduced to non-psychological states. Nevertheless, although Janet (1907a) rightly rejects postulating non-conscious "unconscious" mental states, he appears to sit comfortably with the descriptive sense of unconscious mentality (Janet, 1907b). For example, we find in Janet's writing that the hysteric subject is neither aware of the fixed ideas nor the associated amnesia:

> In hysteria … the amnesia absolute, … [and] the fixed ideas are not expressed, nor even known by the subject. The delirium exists in the mind of the subject without his being conscious of it, and while he goes on talking very reasonably.
> (Janet, 1901, p. 523)

In other words, these fixed ideas exist unknowingly to the principal personality, along with the ignorance of this ignorance. The descriptive view of unconscious mentality is also explicit in the following:

> One understands by an unconscious act an act that has all features of a psychological state or process except that it is not known by the person carrying it out, not even at the moment in which it is carried out.
> (Janet 1888, in and translated by Bühler & Heim, 2009, p. 194)

If this is the case, then Janet is essentially proposing that it is possible to know without knowing or being aware that one knows (i.e., Freud's descriptive view). However, although the descriptive view of unconscious mentality can be coherently formulated, whether there can be multiple knowers is another matter, and as will be shown in the next chapter, accounting for even a single knower brings along with it its own set of challenges.

Summary

Janet and Freud provide the foundations for two main approaches to understanding trauma-dissociation, with the primary distinction relating to deficit and defence, respectively. Janet's deficit account provides a relatively straightforward mechanism for how dissociation arises, but his account neither clearly addresses how dissociation is maintained nor directly explain the origins and basis of multiple knowers. Freud's defence account, on the other hand, has the merit of explaining dissociation as an outcome of the motivated activity of the mind. However, this view suffers explanatory difficulties with respect to addressing how defence is maintained, along with teleological applications in post-Freudian views. There are, nevertheless, similarities between both Janet's and Freud's accounts, although the possibility of multiple knowers requires further consideration for understanding how these positions inform our understanding of personality in DID.

Notes

1 It is worth briefly pointing out that the self or ego is typically seen as a conscious agency, and sometimes equated with 'consciousness', which potentially conflates the knower with the act of knowing.
2 Janet here remarks: the "suggestion is always an idea *isolated* from the great mass of the other thoughts; it has an *independent* development" (Janet, 1901, pp. 266–267, italics in original).
3 "*Dédoublement*" is translated as "undoubling" in Janet (1901), a term that might typically connote a reversing of doubling such that what were two become one. However, as in the context cited above, it is clear that "undoubling" here refers to splitting into two rather than the reverse.
4 There is ongoing debate about the precise relation of repression to defence (see Boag, 2017 for discussion). Here is not the place to resolve such terminological disputes, but repression as motivated ignorance might be seen as a species of the broader concept of defence, the latter referring to any self-protective (psychological) action.
5 First mentioned in a letter to Fliess dated September 21, 1897 (Freud in Masson, 1985). Frampton (1991) observes, however, that public denouncement did not occur until 1906 (Freud, 1906a).
6 Many current psychodynamic positions associate repression with the non-declarative cognitive unconscious, where mental content fails to ever become declaratively conscious, and so do not need to be actively repressed. These accounts are not directly relevant to the present discussion, but for a critique of these positions, see Boag (2019).
7 Wilkie et al. (2007) further note that "autotomy" has more recently come to simply mean self-mutilation. Given that this more recent position develops later in the 20th century, it is safe to conclude that Janet's meaning can be interpreted in light of Fredericq's usage.
8 Intentional action here might be taken to mean action guided by desire and belief.

Chapter 5

On the nature of dissociative parts

The previous chapter drew attention to questions concerning the possibility of multiple knowers, and one immediate challenge with making sense of dissociation and DID is that it challenges the common-sense view of persons. In this respect, Kihlstrom (2005) writes that the dissociative disorders raise "fundamental questions concerning consciousness, identity, the self, and the unity of the person" (p. 241). Dorahy et al. (2014) go so far as to write that "DID questions the concept of self as an autonomous and integrated entity, and thus challenges understanding of the nature of scientific enquiry itself" (p. 412). What it means to be a "person" is, however, rather nebulous, although it is typically taken to be a peculiarly human predicate referring to an intelligent, rational, self-conscious agent (see Dennett, 1988). Conceived of as such, a case could be made that the personality parts in DID appear to *prima facie* satisfy such criteria for personhood since they possess a certain cognitive autonomy and self-reflectiveness. Şar et al. (2017), for instance, write that "each of these identities reports their own subjective experiences and memories, their own sense of agency and will, and their own perspective on who they are" (p. 138). If so, then this would seem to indicate that each personality part is self-reflective and has sufficient complexity for making independent decisions, in the same way that any other "person" might.

The situation is not so clear cut, however, since not everyone agrees that the parts found in DID are distinct "personalities". Morton Prince (1906), for example, initially describes the dissociative parts in the case of Miss Beauchamp as "several distinct people", each possessing an individual character (p. 2). He nevertheless goes on to state, that rather than using the term "multiple personality", "a more correct term is *disintegrated* personality, for each secondary personality is a part only of a normal whole self" (p. 3, italics in original). As already mentioned in the introduction, Prince's position is echoed by various other authors (e.g., Dalenberg et al. 2012; Spiegel, 2006; Spiegel et al., 2013). At the same time, it is difficult to assess such claims because what is taken to be the whole person (or self, and so on) is rarely, if ever, discussed. Prince (1906), for instance, writes that with DID, "certain mental states have been dissociated from the main stream of consciousness and have acquired a more or less independent existence, and formed an *extra* mind" (p. 17, italics in original). However, what to make of this "main stream of

DOI: 10.4324/9781003328254-5

consciousness" and how it relates to an "extra mind" is left up to the reader to intuitively grasp. Consequently, how the dissociative parts relate to the greater personality or "whole self", whatever that might be, remains unclear.

Nevertheless, addressing such terms is critical for making sense of DID, and, as such, the aim of the present chapter is to examine the nature of personality and dissociative parts and address how these relate to both the self and identity. The chapter begins by addressing the common-sense view of the self, along with problems associated with proposing a unified singular agency. These problems provide grounds for a set of requirements that any account of personality, singular or multiple, must satisfy. The chapter then addresses objections to mental plurality before discussing the logical requirements for postulating knowers in the context of strong partitioning. The structural theory of dissociation and its contribution to understanding personality multiplicity is then examined, and a preliminary case made for substantiating the knowers via the action systems identified in affective neuroscience. On the proposal here, the structural theory provides a coherent platform for understanding dissociative parts, where by the basic knowing subjects underlying personality are the action systems, who through competition and collaboration identify with various roles, in either any singular or multiple sense of selves (cf. Maze, 1983).

What is the self? Self-as-subject and self-as-object

If dissociative parts are not to be taken as individual "personalities", then a good place to start concerns what is meant by the "normal whole self" (Prince, 1906, p. 3). In this respect, a long-standing common-sense position holds that each individual consists of a single knowing agent (a "self" or ego), which is then typically taken to be the agent that guides and directs activity (Bertocci, 1945).[1] This belief in a single unified knower or "self" is generally taken to be phenomenologically indisputable and reflect a core reality within human psychology. Some even claim that "[t]he nature of the self is at the heart of psychology" (Strohminger, Knobe & Newman, 2017, p. 551).

Whatever this self might be, however, is not entirely clear, and the situation is not helped by the wide variety of "self"-prefixed concepts found within the literature (e.g., self-regulation, self-awareness, self-acceptance, self-monitoring, self-confidence, self-concept, self-esteem, self-efficacy, self-control, etc.). In fact, Sleeth (2006) here writes that the sheer prevalence of self-related terms in the literature means that the "self has come to mean so many things that it hardly means anything at all" (p. 243). Nevertheless, in line with the conceptual framework developed in Chapter 2, the first approach here for making sense of the self might be to distinguish between the self-as-subject and self-as-object. McAdams (2013), in this respect, recognises an important distinction here between the "Observing I" and the observed "Me" (p. 273; cf. James, 1890), corresponding to the self as the knowing subject term, and the known self-as-object term. On this view, the self-as-subject is a knower that observes and regulates itself via self-reflection, and it is this

"Observing I" that reflects upon the observed "Me" (self-as-object). Thus, we can logically distinguish between self-as-subject and the self-as-object, whereby the self-as-object is typically taken to be a self-representation, standing as the object of cognition in the self-cognising relation. Many authors, in fact, reserve the term self for the self-as-object. Klein (2010), for instance, defines the self essentially in terms of the *object* of experience, where the experienced self entails knowledge and memories of oneself, or the experience of a sense of agency and ownership. Lambie and Marcel (2002) similarly treat the self as "the content of experience, that is, a phenomenal object" (p. 231). On such accounts, to have multiple selves would be akin to simply having multiple perspectives concerning oneself (cf. McConell, 2011).[2]

Other authors, however, focus on the self-as-subject, whereby the self is held responsible for making decisions and controlling behaviour (cf. Allport, 1961). In this sense, the self is an agent—a knowing doer—that instigates action. Baumeister et al. (2018), for instance, write that they use both self and "agency" "in the sense of one who takes action rather than in the sense of representing someone else. The self is, among other things, one who acts..." (p. 38). Taken as such, the self-as-subject is a conscious or self-reflective agent instigating its own activity, and so a reasonable question to ask concerns what this knowing agent specifically is. However, here we encounter a problem since this agentic "self" is typically discussed only in terms of what it *does*, rather than what it *is*. Consider, for example, McAdams's (2013) "actor-agent-author" framework for understanding the self's relationship to itself and others. Here the self is either characterised in terms of its roles (e.g., a "social actor" or "autobiographical author"), which are essentially descriptions of what any such agent might be said to do. Alternatively, when McAdams describes the "self as a reflexive arrangement of the observing I and the to-be-observed Me" (p. 273), he characterises the self as a relation (a reflexive arrangement between the I and the me) rather than in terms of a self-as-subject with its own intrinsic feature. As developed in Chapter 2, if the self is said to both somehow stand as an agent, and yet, is only characterised by what it is said to do, then we have an instance of reification, *viz.* "to treat relations as if they were terms, entities possessing independent natures of their own" (McMullen, 1996, p. 61). Klein (2010) summarises the theoretical situation:

> [t]he phenomenology is universal. Each of us has the experience of a unitary self, an 'I' that remembers, chooses, thinks, plans, and feels. Yet it has been notoriously difficult to provide an account of just what this thinking, feeling, remembering, and planning entity is.
>
> (p. 172)

Explaining how the self acts is also not straightforward. If the self is an agent that makes decisions and initiates action, then it will need to be sufficiently complex and connected to motivational and perceptual systems if it is to play any explanatory role. In this respect, the self would need to be more than a homunculus (or little person) that simply self-determines course of action. Otherwise, as Wegner (2005) rightfully notes, such a homunculus simply defers explanation: "Whenever we explain a behaviour by saying that some personlike agent inside the person simply caused it, we have imagined a homunculus and have thereby committed a classic error of psychological explanation" (*viz.* "the homunculus must itself be explained"—p. 20). However, it is not uncommon to see the explanatory role of the self typically attributed to self-determination. McAdams (2013), for instance, writes, "[t]o be an agent is to make choices and, as a result of those choices, to move forward in life in a self-determined and goal-directed manner" (p. 276). In this regard, Martin, Sugarman, and Thompson (2003) write that human agency

> refers to the deliberative, reflecting activity of a human being in selecting, framing, choosing, and executing his or her actions in a way that is not fully determined by factors and conditions other than his or her own understanding and reasoning.
>
> (p. 112)

What is precisely meant by "not fully determined by factors and conditions other than his or her own understanding and reasoning" is not entirely clear, but if taken to mean that the agent can somehow make decisions independent of causal circumstances, then we are left with the situation whereby "the homunculus causes things merely by deciding, without any prior causes leading to these decisions" (Wegner, 2005, p. 20). Such a position would make behaviour literally inexplicable (i.e., this position rules out the possibility of a science of psychology; Maze, 1983, 1987), and so is presumably not the intended meaning. However, such considerations draw attention to the fact that such accounts lack any serious explanatory account of the self-as-agent.

As developed in Chapter 2, neither reflection nor fore-thought are incompatible with causal explanation since such variables can stand as causal antecedents (Maze, 1983). Nevertheless, as previously discussed, such psychological acts must form part of a causal network involving motivation and affective states. This is simply because cognition is policy neutral and alone cannot explain why one person acts upon the belief and why another person does not (e.g., Boag, 2012, 2017; Maze, 1983, 1987; Mackay, 1996, 1997). Instead, a motivational component (i.e., "desiring") is needed to explain a given person's policy regarding how he or she acts on that belief. Explaining action thus requires an account of what *moves* or drives behaviour (cf. Dweck, 2017), both in sense of the causal factors underlying behaviour, as well as the determinants of the direction of such activity (e.g., goals; Mackay, 1996, 1997; Maze, 1983).

Consequently, any serious explanatory role for the self-as-agent will necessarily require a substantive theory of motivation for addressing the determinants of actions. In this regard, any satisfactory account must address the causal antecedents and interactions giving rise to apparent goal-seeking behaviour (Boag, 2017; Mackay, 1996; Maze, 1983), which will necessarily include (although not be limited to) complex anatomical structures and biochemical processes. In this respect,

Baumeister et al. (2018) are headed in the right direction when they claim that "[h]uman selfhood is a rich, complex organization of psychological and biological processes" (Baumeister et al., 2018, p. 45), and that as part of its adaptive function, "the human self has evolved cognitive and motivational structures" (p. 36). Be this as it may, their claim is still only an in-principle argument rather than a substantive one. What instead is required is a clear account of what the self specifically is, along with the motivational sources of human action that determine its activity.

In summary, given that the self is typically left uncharacterised and without sufficient grounds for explaining human activity, then the clear way forward is to identify the intrinsic features of any such agent (or agents), as well as to provide a coherent explanatory account of any such agent's activity. In the latter respect, any comprehensive general theory of personality must address how any apparent agency is related to biologically based motivational, affective, and cognitive processes.

Justification for postulating multiple knowers

If there are theoretical difficulties associated with substantiating the self, proposing multiple knowers might appear then to simply multiply the problem of addressing a knowing agent. "Strongly" partitive accounts of mind, however, propose that the mind is inhabited by a multiplicity of knowers, which are sometimes invoked to explain how phenomena such as self-deception and akrasia might be possible (e.g., Cavell, 1993; Heil, 1989). For example, in the case of holding contradictory beliefs, rather than attempting to understand how a single agent can simultaneously believe that *p* and believe that not-*p*, the contradictory beliefs are partitioned: the beliefs are said to be held by different "parts" of the mind. Strong partitioning is also invoked for explaining conflict and psychological defence. Maze (1983), for example, writes that

> [i]t is only from a pluralistic view …that one can begin to make sense of the facts of internal conflict and of repression, of the situation in which one part of the psychological apparatus knows something that another part does not know.
> (Maze, 1983, p. 162).

Whether strong partitioning is required for explaining either contradictory beliefs or psychological conflict is, of course, open to dispute and various authors nevertheless believe that any apparent multiplicity of minds can be explained sufficiently with reference to a single mind (i.e., multiplicity is not necessary for accounting for apparent multiplicity; cf. Freud, 1915e). Gardner (1993), for instance, argues that being in "two minds" or conflicted about something can nevertheless be comprehensible within the context of single mind: "Persons do have parts, in the sense that their personalities comprehend contrasting sources of motivation: but not in the sense that their minds have parts which function like agents" (p. 78). Be this as it may, if the "person" acts as an executive, arbitrating between different desires, then this agent must also be motivated (i.e., have its own desires) to explain how they arbitrate between one course of action and another (see Maze, 1983, 1987; Michell, 1988). If so, there are then, by implication, at least two poles of agency consisting of "person desires" and "non-person desires", given that any desire requires a desirer (*viz.* a subject term). Consequently, to say that a "person" manages his or her "conflict-ing desires" requires both the person, as subject, desiring to manage their conflicting desires, along with the subject(s) of the conflicting desires. Consequently, postulat-ing a "person" managing conflicting desires simply multiplies the number of know-ers involved, rather than pointing to a single agent as first presumed.

There are, nevertheless, a number of objections to strong partitioning, including inventing knowing subsystems *ad hoc* and *ad libitum* to explain certain phenom-ena. These problems regularly occurs in cases where strong partitioning is invoked to address phenomena such as self-deception (e.g., Pears, 1986; see Boag, 2005 for critical discussion). To address this, one might simply posit that subsystems cannot simply arise *ex nihilo* for the sake of fulfilling a function, and that their origins must be explicable within a deterministic framework (i.e., we must specify the condi-tions from which these subsystems arise). Nevertheless, "the problem remains of how one is to specify and justify any particular theoretical division as opposed to any other" (Neu, 1988, p. 88) and Bucci (2016) here notes that there are two main directions: some theories assume a unified personality to begin with, and then try to account for multiplicity, whereas other theories assume that personality begins as an initial multiplicity and so any apparent unity then needs to be accounted for. In either case, Gardner (1993) observes that any account of subsystems remains prob-lematic unless a coherent and parsimonious account of their origins is provided. He does, however, provide an example of what he considers to be satisfactory:

> One possibility remains. It is that sub-systems are always present in human personality, in some actual or immanent form. To say this would be to claim that, from manifest mental disunity in certain contexts, the concealed existence of two or more mind-like entities at all times is to be inferred. This would solve the problem of causal genesis: if rational existence is in fact no different funda-mentally, no special explanation is owed for the appearance of sub-systems in irrationality.
>
> (p. 76)

If Gardner here is correct, then furnishing a satisfactory account of the origins of subsystems within normal psychology surmounts one hurdle to a coherent account of multiplicity.

Dissociative parts and the mereological fallacy

One other potential problem for postulating strong partitioning concerns the mere-ological fallacy. Although not a logical fallacy *per se*, the mistake involves erro-neously ascribing psychological predicates to functional parts of a whole system, when such predicates instead should only apply to the whole system (e.g., the living organism) (Bennet & Hacker, 2003; Smit & Hacker, 2014). By way of example, Smit and Hacker (2014) write,

> it makes sense to say that the animal as a whole has a memory, is able to retain information, and possesses knowledge, but it makes no sense to say that for example the hippocampus or cortex possesses knowledge. It is the animal as a whole that retains information and exercises the ability to retain information, not its parts.
>
> (p. 1079)

Consequently, claims such as "the brain experiences *x*" or "the brain believes *y*" should instead be phrased as "the person experiences *x*" or the "person believes *y*" since "psychological predicates apply paradigmatically to the *human being (or animal) as a whole*, and *not* to the body or its parts" (Bennett & Hacker, 2003, p. 73, italics in original). Bennett and Hacker (2003) here write:

> The brain neither sees, *nor is it blind*—just as sticks and stones are not awake, *but they are not asleep either*. The brain makes no decisions, but neither is it indecisive. Only what *can* decide can be indecisive. So, too, the brain cannot be conscious; only the living creature whose brain it is can be conscious—or unconscious. *The brain is not a logically appropriate subject for psychological predicates.*
>
> (p. 72, italics in original)

By extension then to DID, postulating knowing personality parts would appear to undermine the notion of the "whole person" and constitute an instance of mereological reduction.

In response, Nijenhuis (2012) writes that the mereological fallacy is itself problematic, since there is no substantive objection to proposing that "the whole system can encompass two or more subsystems that each have goals and that each engage in explicit goal-directed behaviour" (p. 114). After all, we know that there are functionally independent subsystems evident in brain architecture (e.g., Panksepp, 2005; Panksepp & Biven, 2012). Nijenhuis instead proposes then that any dissociative part need only be connected to the greater personality constituting the whole system. As discussed below, this position has merit since the mereological fallacy makes assumptions about the whole system being necessary for substantiating the knowing subject. In fact, to argue paradigmatically that only entire persons or organisms can engage in psychological acts simply eliminates the possibility of mental plurality *a priori*. Moreover, as the earlier analysis indicates, explaining behaviour at the level of the "person" is also potentially problematic since the person then appears to decide and act rationally (freely even). As such, the claim that the brain evaluates and "decides" is no more problematic than attributing decision-making and evaluation to the "person": in both cases some mechanistic account must be provided to make such a claim intelligible (i.e., something greater than "choosing" must be posited to avoid explanatory vacuity).

Bennett and Hacker (2003) do nevertheless draw attention to a legitimate problem in terms of part-whole relations: not *all* parts can be expected to be capable of standing within cognitive relations. However, in contradiction to these authors, this is, in fact, primarily an empirical issue with respect to whether any particular (sub) system is capable of engaging in psychological relations. The relevant question should rather be then whether some structure X *has the necessary and sufficient conditions for psychological activity* when considering claims about knowing brain parts (Boag, 2012). For this reason, it would be wrong to state that a single neuron might constitute a knower, although a set of structures in the brain with sufficient complexity might. What counts as "sufficient complexity" is, of course, difficult to determine,[3] but there is no apparent logical objection to positing psychobiological subsystems that can each engage cognitively with the environment, if each is sufficiently connected to the perceptual system to allow cognitive sensitivity to the environment (Maze, 1983).

Which criteria must a strongly partitive account satisfy?

As discussed above, to simply ascribe knowing to the entire organism is to *a priori* eliminate the possibility of mental plurality, which simply presupposes an answer to the issue under investigation. Additionally, postulating multiple knowers provides no greater grounds for theoretical concern than that of postulating a single knower: any proposed knower must possess its own intrinsic qualities and consequently be capable of characterisation independently of the activities it is said to enter into (cf. Maze, 1983). Furthermore, any theory must provide a satisfactory account of the origins of any such knowing subsystems (cf. Gardner, 1993). These factors alone are not sufficient, however, since the dissociative personality parts are typically also ascribed agency (i.e., are viewed as both doers and knowers), and so some account of their motivational, cognitive, and affective policy requires addressing (cf. Boag, 2018).

Taking the above into consideration, any theory of dissociative parts must coherently address the following:

i. Given that dissociative parts are said to be both knowers and doers (e.g., Van der Hart et al., 2006), then any theory must substantiate what stands as the subject term of the knowing and doing relation. Consequently, this requires characterising these subjects independently of what they are said to do.
ii. Given that dissociative parts are both motivated and appear to independently think and feel, then any theory must provide a coherent account of the part's motivational, affective, and cognitive policies through their connection to these systems.
iii. The origins of any proposed dissociative parts need to be coherently accounted for.

A further challenge to making sense of personality parts in DID is both substantiating the subject terms while also addressing the phenomenological character of DID. The specific challenge here is accounting for the apparent fluidity of parts with respect to how independent multiple knowers can seemingly arise, disappear, and also merge with one another (Steele et al., 2014b). Given this, the specific challenge then is addressing how the dissociative parts can both be substantive knowing subjects, while also addressing how these parts also appear to arise, blend, or even dissolve. By extension, the role of culture needs to be addressed, especially with respect to the various cultural manifestations of DID, including possession states (cf. DSM-5; APA, 2013).

Theories of dissociative parts

Judging whether any theory of personality parts in DID meet the requirements for strong partitioning is not straightforward, however. For a start, there is inconsistent terminology used to describe dissociative parts (e.g., "alters"—Kluft, 2006; Manning & Manning, 2007; Özturk & Şar, 2016; "self-states"—Dorahy et al., 2014), and the relation of these dissociative parts to other personality structures such as "ego-states" is not always clear (e.g., Nijenhuis, 2015, 2019; Ross, 2014). Nevertheless, it is clear that in many cases dissociated personality parts assume the role of individual knowing subjects since such "multiple 'I' selves" are taken to each have "their own unique perspective on the world and who they are", co-existing within a single individual (Şar, Dorahy & Krüger, 2017, p. 138). For example, Kluft (2006) reports that dissociative parts (alters) "have their own identities, involving a sense of self (a center of initiative and experience)" along with "a characteristic self-representation, which may be discordant with how the patient is generally seen or perceived" (p. 284). Moreover, the personality parts concurrently hold different perspectives and take ownership of their actions, such that they

> have their own senses of autobiographical memory, distinguishing what they understand to be their own actions and experiences from those done and experienced by other alters; and … have a sense of ownership of their own experiences, actions, and thoughts, and may lack a sense of ownership of and a sense of responsibility for the action, experiences, and thoughts of other alters.
>
> (Kluft, 2006, p. 284)

Additionally, dissociated personality parts have a certain person-level complexity, with Manning and Manning (2007) reporting that the dissociative personality parts "differ in their attitudes and dispositions. Some, for example, may be religious, others atheist. Some may love a person, others hate him or her. Some may be trusting, others suspicious" (p. 842).

One example of strong partitioning that fails to meet the criteria above is "Legion Theory" (Manning & Manning, 2007). Legion theory proposes multiple selves, whereby each self is both an independent knower and agent: "Each of the selves possesses its own set of memories and has its own disposition. At any point in time a single self will have control of the body, or will dominate the actions of the body" (p. 846). Such selves concurrently experience one and the same event, such that "selves will have separate, and differing, memories of the same events as viewed from their different dispositions and perspectives" (p. 846). Here, the authors compare the selves to individual perceptual streams, writing that

> [i]n a manner analogous to the parallel visual systems driven by the left and right eyes integrating to form a unified binocular visual system, we propose the existence of parallel cognitive/personality/memory streams, which we call selves, working together in an integrated manner to form a unified personality system, which we call the corporate self.
>
> (p. 845)

Manning and Manning offer no constraint on the number of possible selves, and in terms of their origin, we learn that these "[s]elves are innate—part of our genetic structure. The infant arrives with a handful of selves" (p. 848).

At the same time, however, these selves are somehow disembodied, with the authors writing that it is near impossible to conceptualise multiple knowers within a single body:

> [w]ith a body-centred perspective, the concept of DID is difficult to conceive 'How can there be multiple selves when there is only one body?' Locked into this perspective, the existence of multiple personalities within a single person is almost unthinkable.
>
> (Manning & Manning, 2007, p. 845)

Instead, Manning and Manning believe that these selves inhabit some type of psychological rather bodily space. One immediate problem here, however, is that these selves are left uncharacterised—we are only told what the selves do, rather than what they are—and there is no attempt to connect such selves to motivational and affective processes. Furthermore, the metaphoric comparison of selves with parallel streams of visual processing (p. 854) is unhelpful, because such unidimensional processing neither captures the complexity of dissociative parts, nor the connection of selves to motivation and affects, even though such selves are clearly interested in the world around them. For example, Manning and Manning (2007) explain switches of executive control with respect to "interest in the situation":

> ... the particular self which has executive control at a particular time would ordinarily be the self with the greatest interest in the situation and, therefore, would be most likely to best remember the situation. We know from selves which are alters that selves have different interests and will perform different

functions (studying, socializing, parenting, etc.). So for a particular individual, we would expect the same self to usually have executive control in heated arguments, another self to have control when performing tasks at work, and still another self to have control when dealing with children.

(p. 851)

However, without characterising the selves, we are in no position to know what these selves and their interests might be, and so this particular theoretical position is problematic in any explanatory sense. The theory simply asserts that strong partitioning holds, without any way of determining whether the theory has any bearing upon reality. As a result, multiple selves can be potentially postulated both *ad hoc* and *ad libitum*, with no way of determining which selves exist, along with no clear distinction between subject and object term, and no meaningful connection to either motivational or affective states and their policies.

Other potentially problematic examples of dissociative parts are found when the distinction between subject and object is not always kept clearly in focus. For instance, Pica (1999) proposes that in the case of DID, the dissociated personality parts are essentially elaborate imaginary companions. According to Pica, these imaginary companions first arise in response to coping with unpleasant affect, before then "filling in" for the child during situations of distress. DID then finally emerges when the imaginary companions "are transformed into distinct personality states that have become invested in their separateness, and think of themselves as autonomous entities" (pp. 411–412). As might be apparent, imaginary friends begin as objects of the child's imagination but then somehow metamorphise into independent knowers—subject terms—each with their own perspective. Thus, an important question that such an account must address concerns how something that is first an *object* of cognition becomes a knowing *subject* able to take objects, and with its own motives, viewpoint, and so on.[4]

Similar questions are raised in Özturk and Şar's (2016) account, who propose that dissociative parts are independent knowers that arise out of multiple perspectives held during a traumatising event. Here, these authors write that "the subject evaluates himself or herself… and the traumatic experience from diverse perspectives" (p. 2), such that a single knowing subject initially has various evaluative viewpoints of the situation ("the subject evaluates himself or herself"). However, these perspectives then emerge as independent perceivers such that "each alter personality has independent and different judgements about these internal and external processes": "These perceptions about oneself which originate from diverse perspectives, aggregate around multiple foci. Related emotions, thoughts, and behaviour styles are linked to these foci over time. These aggregates become alter personalities following repeated utilization" (p. 2). So, and as with Pica above, the relevant question concerns how what are essentially first *objects* of cognition (i.e., something known) become then transformed into *subjects* engaging in cognitive acts with those same objects.

An example that meets the logical requirements of strong partitioning

The latter examples above may not necessarily be problematic (a plausible mechanism may still be forthcoming), but as the positions currently stand, there is not a clear mechanism for explaining how something known can become a knower, with its own motivational bases, and so on. An example of strong partitioning, on the other hand, that addresses such issues is Maze's (1983, 1987) strongly partitive account emerging from Freudian theory. In Maze's proposal, the smallest knowing units within the organism are the psychobiological motivational "drive" structures, which, via the nervous system, come to know states of affairs relevant to learnt sources of gratification and frustration. Here, Maze extends upon the Freudian concept of "instinctual drives" (*Triebe*),[5] and he proposes a position broadly consistent with what is currently known concerning (homeostatic) drives (e.g., Berridge, 2004). Although the matter needs to be resolved empirically, a provisional list of drives identified via exciting and satiating biochemical events (and identifiable consummatory actions) includes sexuality (or several specific sexualities), hunger (or several specific hungers), thirst, a respiratory drive, pain avoidance (where pain is specified by literal activation of pain nerves, and the satiating behaviour anything that terminates that activation), and a temperature control drive, specified similarly to pain avoidance (Maze, 1983).[6]

Maze extends upon Freud's (1915c) recognition that motivational drives are *psychobiological* systems by proposing that these drives engage cognitively with the environment in their quest for gratification and avoidance of frustration. By way of example, the hunger drive instigates awareness of available food sources, activates motor systems related to locating food and ingestion, while also being sensitive to metabolic feedback involved in eating. However, rather than anthropomorphic homunculi ("little persons"), each drive is a biomechanical systems utilising cognition. Maze's position is thus consistent with the view that cognition is in the service of the motivational/affective systems. Wright and Panksepp (2012), for example, write:

> The underlying forces of the mind, which were intrinsically motivational, now provide the future orientation needed for planning and the coherence for more explicit ideas in the mind, and a much more focused experience of motivation emerges, which still has intrinsic and often compelling urges to be enacted but also allows for the experience and analysis of other competing or alternative motivations.
>
> (p. 24)

In a related fashion, Mackay (2002) writes that "drives are the engines of action, and cognitions are the servants of the passions" (p. 6), and given that there are multiple motivational systems, Maze proposes then that each individual is made up of a small community of these drives, "each of which is a knower and a doer" (Maze, 1987,

p. 197). Of course, and as noted in the previous chapter, Freud explicitly rejects the possibility of multiple knowers (Freud, 1912g, 1915e). However, the possibility and indeed theoretical necessity of multiple knowers is nonetheless implicated in Freudian theory given both that motivational conflict implies division and that drives cannot be "blind bodily forces" (Maze, 1983; see also Boag, 2005, 2014, 2017).

In terms of meeting the requirements for strong partitioning, one advantage of Maze's account is that it circumvents both the homunculi objection and criticisms concerning the gratuitous postulation of subagencies *ad hoc* and *ad libitum*. Specifically, Freud (1915c) proposes that drives must be identified by their organic *sources*, rather than by their apparent *aims*, the former providing an "in-principle" method for identifying the knowing subjects within the confines of the organism's physical structure. As physical structures, the drives can be characterised independently of the relations that they are said to enter into, and their number and specification are ultimately resolved empirically. Furthermore, these drives are present at birth and can be seen to originate through the history of the evolution of the physical organism. Maze's (1983) position is also consistent with efficient causation since rather than constituting "whole persons", these drives are subsets of neural structures (biomechanical systems) that simply operate via their in-built motivational and affective policies. This means that each drive here is simply a mechanistic system (literally a psychobiological engine) that, once activated, impels the organism's cognitive-behavioural activity until other factors intervene to terminate or arrest that activity (e.g., gratification; motivational conflict; and repression) (Maze, 1983; see also Boag, 2005). Rather than constituting homunculi, once activated, these action systems are thoroughly "self-serving" in relation to their biologically wired interests and learnt sources of gratification and frustration:

> …unlike the whole person each has, in effect, only one motive, never restrains itself from seeking satisfaction, knows only a portion of the aggregate body of information, and suffers no internal conflict. An instinctual drive can no more restrain itself from working than any motor can, once the switches are thrown. If its operation is to be arrested, then that must be through some influence external to itself—in the case of repression, from other instinctual drives.
>
> (Maze, 1987, p. 197)

As such, rather than a "person" (or self) acting rationally and deciding upon when and how to act, the behaviour of the "whole person" thus results from both facilitating and inhibiting influences emerging from the interaction of these drives and their interaction with the world around them. The apparent unity of the person and any singular sense of identity could follow from a drive neither knowing itself directly (nor the other drives) and instead only knowing and identifying with the *whole* organism and its activities (Boag, 2005). Social interactions and roles would presumably further reinforce the development of this more or less coherent sense of self since we appear as a single organism to others and are treated as such accordingly. Taken together, "[t]he resulting belief of a unified self is as *prima facie* plausible as the belief that the sun revolves around the earth" (Boag, 2005, p. 753). Nevertheless, the known self, ostensibly acting as the agent behind action, is essentially a fantasy—a false belief—based upon appearances (cf. Grossman, 1982). How such an account might address multiple selves is discussed further below.

The structural theory and dissociative parts

Within theories of dissociation, the structural theory provides the most clearly articulated and sophisticated discussion of dissociative parts. The dissociative parts are each taken to be knowers standing in various cognitive, affective, and behavioural relations: "divisions (or dissociations) of the personality (consciousness) implies the existence of two or more dissociative psychobiological systems, each with its own collection of memories, affective experiences, behavioral repertoires, and sense of self" (Dorahy & Van der Hart, 2007, p. 6). The structural theory of dissociation similarly proposes that the dissociative parts each possess their own sense of consciousness and so appear to be individual knowers that can take themselves as objects (Steele et al. 2014a; Van der Hart, Van Dijke, Van Son & Steele, 2000; Van der Hart et al., 2006): "Each part includes at least a rudimentary sense of an experiencing 'I'" (Steele et al., 2014b, p. 242), which includes to varying degrees a knowing subject holding an independent sense of self:

> We describe the division of personality in terms of *dissociative parts of the personality*. This choice of term emphasizes the fact that dissociative parts of the personality constitute one whole, yet are self-conscious, have at least a rudimentary sense of self, and are generally more complex than a single psychobiological state.
>
> (Van der Hart et al., 2006, p. 4, italics in original)

That these are distinct knowers is also made explicit by Nijenhuis (2012, 2015), who has contributed the most here philosophically for understanding the nature of mind within structural dissociation. Nijenhuis (2015) explicitly contrasts the distinction between a single knower experiencing conflict with multiple knowers found in structural dissociation, writing that

> [e]xperiencing conflict between two wills that an individual regards as his or her own is phenomenologically very different from experiencing a conflict between an ANP and a fragile EP and a controlling EP—or being flooded by feelings, thoughts, images, or behaviors that stem from one or more dissociative parts that the engulfed dissociative part is now aware of.
>
> (p. 62)

Instead, each dissociative part stands as a subject term standing in the knowing relation: "The cardinal feature of patients with dissociative disorders is that they involve multiple first-person perspectives" (Nijenhuis, 2012, p. 143). Furthermore, not only do the dissociative parts stand as knowers, these personality parts are also self-aware and "experience a phenomenal self" (Nijenhuis, 2012, p. 133): "With few exceptions, there parts are convinced that they exist. They experience that they are someone, that they are a subject" (Nijenhuis, 2012, p. 141). Each dissociative part "decides, thinks or feels something" (Nijenhuis, 2012, p. 114) and is also capable of distinct, independent experiences across time: "[m]ost dissociative parts experience that they remain the same 'person' across time, also when they in fact change to a degree" (Nijenhuis, 2012, p. 132). Taking these points together, the structural theory of dissociation proposes that these dissociative parts, to varying degrees, express full phenomenology of self-hood, such that each part would appear to qualify as a "person", as generally conceived (cf. Dennett, 1988).

The structural theory and the origins of dissociative parts

The structural theory proposes an account of the origins of the knowing systems that bears some similarity to Maze's (1983) described above. According to the structural theory, the "[a]ction systems are the basic elements that shape personality" (Van der Hart et al., 2006, p. 33), and these action systems appear to constitute the basic knowing units of personality since they are "self-conscious psychobiological systems" (Van der Hart et al., 2006, p. 31). In terms of their origins, these systems have been shaped by evolution to serve survival and reproductive functions and underlie an individual's cognitive, affective, and motivational processes: "Action systems manifest as patterns of activation in sensory awareness, perceptual bias, emotional tone, emotional regulation, memory processes, mental models, behavioural response patterns..., and in humans, a sense of self" (Steele et al., 2014b, p. 243). Thus, much like Maze's (1983) account of the Freudian drives (Freud, 1915c), these action systems are comprehensible within an evolutionary framework and comprise systems that help maintain survival and reproduction: "Their purpose is to generate affective feelings that help animals and humans to (1) determine whether an event is biologically useful or harmful, and (2) evoke adaptive responses to current life circumstances" (Steele et al., 2014b, p. 243). Given that there are numerous action systems, "personality can be understood as a certain constellation of action systems" (Nijenhuis, 2012, p. 129) and it is these same systems that underlie the dissociative parts: "[t]hese dissociative parts are mediated by action systems" (Van der Hart et al., 2006, p. 4).

Grounding personality in action systems provides a means for substantiating the subject term underlying dissociative parts, as well as accounting for their motivational and affective policy. As Nijenhuis (2012) writes, "action system are major organizers of attention, cognition and behavioural action. They guide what is to be integrated and ignored, and what is to be pursued" (p.139; cf. Nijenhuis, 2015, 2019). Essentially, then, the action systems are responsible for what we think, feel, and do: "Action subsystems guide individual to notice and be drawn to particular kinds of stimuli and shape the action tendencies in which they engage" (Van der Hart et al., 2006, p. 33). As with Maze's (1983) account, however, these action systems "do not compel an individual to act in a fixed way" (Steele et al., 2014b, p. 243). Instead, these systems engage in complex behaviours that are sensitive to environmental circumstances. For example, the hunger system performs actions such as noticing and obtaining food, rather than simply "eating", since other actions are required for executing their activities (e.g., walking somewhere to obtain food). As Van der Hart et al. (2006) write: "It should be noted that most action tendencies are not specific to a given action system or its component but can be modified and 'plugged in' to achieve a variety of goals. For example, different action systems can promote running to achieve a goal. An individual can run from threat and toward a safe place (defense), run in a race toward the finish line (play), and run toward a loved one (attachment)" (p. 34).

The benefit of grounding personality and dissociative parts within the action systems is that these parts can be understood as evolutionary-shaped systems: "They are evolutionary derived psychophysiological tools for approaching attractive cues or for avoiding aversive stimuli" (Nijenhuis, 2012, p. 129). This means that motivational and affective policies can in principle be formulated, and these systems can learn and modify specific actions relative to feedback and means of achieving motivationally salient outcomes. The plausible origin of action systems follows from Van der Hart et al.'s (2006) proposed set of criteria that any account of action systems must satisfy: (i) these systems must be self-organising and self-stabilising homeostatic systems; (ii) these systems should be comprehensible within a mammalian evolutionarily shaped systems framework; (iii) these systems should be sensitive to classical conditioning; (iv) these systems should be both relatively stable, but also capable of change and individual development; and (v) these systems should be available early on in life.

An empirically based account of action systems that meet these criteria is found in Panksepp's (1998) taxonomy of basic emotions (cf. Steele et al., 2014b). Panksepp and colleagues (e.g., Panksepp, 1998, 2001, 2005; Panksepp & Biven, 2012; Panksepp & Moskal, 2008) identify seven subcortical emotional systems or "basic emotional command systems", which include SEEKING (appetitive foraging), LUST, FEAR (freezing and flight), RAGE, CARE, PANIC/GRIEF (separation distress), and PLAY. The accumulating evidence of multiple affective-motivational neural structures underlying human activity (see Malezieux, Klein & Gogolla, 2023)[7] demonstrates that this approach contributes an important theoretical foundation for understanding the motivational bases underlying personality generally (cf. Maze, 1983). Furthermore, the proposed role of action systems provides a common theoretical platform for both understanding structural dissociation and various psychodynamic perspectives, including those within neuropsychoanalytic fields of enquiry (e.g., Panksepp & Solms, 2012; Panksepp et al., 2019; Solms, 2019, 2020; Solms & Panksepp, 2012; Kernberg, 2022). Action systems provide a clear point of convergence for Janetian and psychodynamic positions.

Are dissociative parts personalities?

Although each dissociative part is said to constitute a relatively independent knower, the structural theory of dissociation nevertheless aims to avoid reifying separate "identities" in such a way that each has independent existence (Steele et al. 2014a; Van der Hart et al., 2006). In this respect, rather than multiple personalities, the structural theory proposes that "[d]issociative parts are components of a single personality" (Van der Hart et al., 2006, p. 30). Here, each knower is taken to simply be a part of the personality system, the latter viewed as a dynamic organisation that develops and changes via interaction with the environment: "Even though dissociative parts have a sense of self, no matter how rudimentary, they are not separate, but rather are different, more or less divided psychobiological systems that are not sufficiently cohesive or coordinated within an individual's personality" (Van der Hart et al., 2006, p. 31).

The structural theory here follows Allport's (1961) definition of personality as a dynamic organisation of psychophysical systems that determines what the person does. Allport, himself, however, proposes this only as a general definition of personality, noting that he is unable to address what these specific psychophysical systems are. In this respect, the role of motivation and affects in Allport's account is left unclear, even if personality "organization entails the functioning of both 'mind' and 'body in some inextricable unity'" (p. 28). What constitutes the knowing subject within Allport's account of the personality system is also unclear, although he states that any such self-as-agent will arise from some currently unspecified system (p. 130). Accordingly, Allport provides little guidance with respect to what this superordinate personality system might actually be, or what constitutes the knowing subject or subjects, or what role motivational and affective processes play.

On the other hand, approaches that postulate a superordinate personality system easily neglect providing a sufficient motivational basis for how such a system operates. For example, Oppenheimer (2002) puts forward an information-monitoring self-system, which he sometimes addresses as something known (i.e., a self-representation), but also treats as a self-organising system that processes information (the "self-as-knower"; p. 105). The role of this self-system is to evaluate, change, and reorganise "contexts and contents relevant for the self ... to form adaptive subsystems that will allow individuals to interact adequately with their environment" (p. 105). However, to determine what information is "relevant" presumably requires that any such self-system has some pre-existing motivational policy to act upon. These bases are presently unaccounted for in Oppenheimer's account, and a lthough one might suggest here that these motivational bases might nevertheless be provided, the more parsimonious position is that the motivational policy are determined by the policies of the foundational action systems. If this position is accepted, then this means, however, that any, such self-system is redundant because the action systems are sufficient for determining motivational policy. Moreover, given that the only evidence for such a self-system is in terms of what it is intended to explain, there is no clear justification for postulating a self or self-system standing over and above the action systems. This further indicates that reserving "personality" for the entire system is of little explanatory value, and so precluding dissociative parts from qualifying as "personalities" has little merit. On the other hand, if "personality can be understood as a certain constellation of action systems", as Nijenhuis (2012, p. 129) believes, then there should be no in-principle objection to viewing each dissociative part as a personality if each represents a specific constellation of action systems.

This latter possibility is buttressed by the recognition that dissociative personality parts in DID are likely composite systems that integrate multiple action systems rather than being composed of a single action system. In relation to this, the structural theory recognises that although "the personality can become divided in an endless number of ways in the context of traumatization" (Nijenhuis, 2012, p. 130), typically, however, a dualistic division occurs whereby "dissociative divisions… primarily take place between the two major categories of psychobiological systems that make up personality" (Van der Hart et al., 2006, p. 3). These two broad categories of action systems are the systems related to sustaining life, relations, and reproduction ("adapting to daily life"), on the one hand, and the systems involved in avoiding and escaping aversive stimuli, on the other. This dualism can be summarised as "(1) those that promote functioning in daily life and survival of the species, and (2) those that serve survival of the individual by promoting defense in the face of threat" (Steele et al., 2014b, p. 243).[8] This provides a metaphorical "natural fault line" for dissociative splits: "Metaphorically speaking, there are natural fault lines between action systems of daily life and those of defense. Under threat, action systems of daily life will be inhibited; in the absence of threat, defense systems will be inhibited" (Steele et al., 2014b, p. 243).

The dissociative parts that form with traumatisation tend to each involve a constellation of action systems rather than a single one. Functionally related action systems (such as attachment and sociability) may be synthesised more readily than non-functionally related ones, including what might be called self-preservative drives that allow functioning in day-to-day life, along with aspects of sexuality. For example, Steele et al. (2014b) write: "The functions of the ANP include exploration of the environment (including work and study), play, energy management (sleeping and eating), attachment, sociability, reproduction/sexuality, and caretaking (especially rearing of children)" (p. 244). This demonstrates that the "daily-life" ANP system is clearly a complex character, since its activities reflect numerous motivational sources. Given this complexity, the use of terms such as personality or personhood does not seem out of order, especially since the action systems associated with the ANP(s) contribute to the larger portion of what someone does.

The dissociative parts associated with EPs, by contrast, do not appear to exhibit such complexity, at least at first glance. EPs are typically grounded in the defensive action systems underlying "mammalian physical defence" (such as separation/attachment cry, hypervigilance, fight, flight, freeze, and submission). According to the structural theory, one EP may be mediated by the flight system (e.g., as in dissociative fugue), while another EP may be mediated by the freeze system, while others may be mediated by systems associated with fight or submission (Steele et al., 2014b). This suggests then that EPs lack complexity and so would lack sufficient character for claiming personhood. Nevertheless, the situation is not so clear cut. Maintaining a sharp division between dissociative parts devoted to daily life and those of defence is unlikely to be successful for several reasons. For one thing, drives such as hunger and thirst have connections with RAGE and FEAR (Kirsch, 2019), suggesting that daily-life functioning is intimately connected with defence.[9] Additionally, if dissociative parts can adapt to situations across time, then they will need to be comprised of a complex assemblage of knowing systems—much in the same way as the ego or self-as-agent is generally taken to be.[10] The simple reason for this is that situations are comprised of varieties of adaptive challenges. It would not be unreasonable then to assume that for ANPs to successfully function in any general sense, there may also be involvement of defensive action systems when circumstances demand. The structural theory, in fact, acknowledges this complexity: "ANPs and EPs are prototypes that have innumerable variations. For example, a part attempts to function at work (ANP daily life action system), but is highly aggressive (fight defense action system)" (Steele et al., 2014b, p. 248).[11] However, this also works the other way around: the dissociative parts constituting the EPs also experience a complex world and exhibit complex motives across time. Consequently, there is no clear argument for not treating dissociative parts as persons or personalities. What we take to be normal personality at any given moment is simply a subset of action systems.

Dissociative parts and the nature of identity

The discussion to this point has only considered the subject term(s) of the knowing relation, and what still requires consideration is the apparent fluidity of parts with respect to how dissociative parts can seemingly arise, disappear, and also merge with one another (Steele et al., 2014b). Here, the nature of "identity" as bound up with the self-as-object requires addressing. The position here is that identity involves an *identifying* relationship whereby minimally, a knowing subject S identifies with some state of affairs y. "Identity" thus is something known—an object of cognition rather than a knowing subject—and so identity can be conceptualised in terms of who or what one perceives oneself to be. William James (1890) long ago observed that all manner of things can be identified with, and one's sense of self and identity can extend outside the boundary of the actual organism to family, possessions, and beyond. Nevertheless, one immediate and relatively common object of identification is the body, even if not always necessarily so. Nijenhuis (2015), following Metzinger (2003), here writes that our conception of self is "strongly body-orientated, perhaps because the body is a steady form of reference" (p. 69), echoing Freud's (1923b) observation that the ego is first and foremost a body ego.

What we identify with, however, also constitutes a relation unfolding across time. In the context of personality, identity involves one's "life story" (or narrative identity) entailing how one identifies with past experiences, the present, and the anticipated future (McAdams, 2001, 2013). Of course, memory plays an essential role throughout (Conway, 2005; Şar et al., 2017). As Şar et al. (2017) write here:

> The development of a sense of self is predicated on the collection of life experiences that are encoded as occurring to the self. Thus the construction of self is underpinned by episodic and semantic autobiographical memories laid down with autonoetic consciousness (i.e., this experience happened to me, and when I remember, it has the felt sense that I experienced it).
>
> (p. 141)

This experience is also largely shaped by one's social interactions, and both advocates and critics of DID agree on the importance of social roles for shaping identity (e.g., Lilienfeld et al., 1999; Spanos, 1994; Steele et al., 2014b). In fact, given that individuals typically hold multiple social roles, various authors observe that we typically develop non-pathological multiple identities or self-representations (e.g., McConnell, 2011; Owens, Robinson & Smith-Lovin, 2010). For example, Stryker's (2008) structural symbolic interactionism theory proposes that any individual develops various identities in relation to social interactions. Stryker here writes, "[i]dentities are ... self-cognitions tied to roles, and through roles, to positions in organized social relationships" (p. 20), which then become hierarchically nested within a salience hierarchy. This hierarchy is "defined as the likelihood that an identity will be invoked in a variety of situations" (Stryker, 2008, p. 20), such that different identities emerge probabilistically in relation to context. Although such theories do not intend to specifically address how dissociative identities might form and be maintained, they do, at minimum, demonstrate that there are theoretical grounds for proposing that any individual may have multiple identities. Extending this to DID, given that any individual performs various roles across different contexts, any assemblage of action systems could potentially construct a sense of self around social roles invoked under certain circumstances (cf. Şar et al., 2017).

The role of culture

The importance of social roles for shaping the sense of self also implicates an important role for culture. As already recognised, there is no necessary tension between the trauma-dissociation and socio-cognitive approaches since there is no logical objection to social factors shaping the expression of the dissociative identities (Dorahy et al., 2014; Şar et al., 2017). Culture is particularly implicated here in shaping social roles, along with beliefs concerning both trauma and identity (Bhavsar et al., 2016; Leising et al., 2009; Moleiro, 2018; Wilson, 2007). As Wilson (2007) observes, "[t]here is no individual experience of psychological trauma without a cultural history, grounding or background. Similarly, there is no individual sense of personal identity without a cultural reference point" (p. 23). In this respect, personality development is always embedded within a cultural context, and one widely recognised distinction holds between individualist-collectivist communities and the respective development of independent and interdependent selves (Markus & Kitayama, 2010)[12]. Such selves will be informed by cultural beliefs, and given that concepts such as "personality" and "identity" are primarily informed by western lines of thinking, DID might manifest differently within other cultural contexts. In relation to this, Dorahy et al. (2014) write, that in non-Western contexts, DID may manifest as *possession states*, whereby the individual gets taken over (i.e., possessed) by some external force, such as a demon or spirit. These authors write: "In African, Asian, and other non-Western countries … DID usually takes the form of pathological possession experiences which are more congruent with a conception of self as not separate or individual" (p. 407). And again: "In certain (e.g., mainstream Western) cultures, [DID] is consonant with a fragmentation of *internal* identities; in other (e.g., non-Western) cultures it may accord with *external* spiritual entities that take control of the individual" (Dorahy et al., 2014, p. 408, their italics). However, the general principle remains the same: it is the action systems identifying with various cultural roles, even if culture might shape the specific expression of identity.

Summary

Any coherent account of DID requires addressing apparent multiple selves and agency, along with addressing the motivational sources and policies embodied within behaviour. The commonly assumed "self-as-agent" is a vague concept that is typically left uncharacterised apart from what it is said to do. As such, accounting for multiple selves is, in principle, no more difficult than accounting for a single self: the subject term or terms need to be substantiated with respect to intrinsic features, along with providing a coherent explanation of the agent's motivational and affective policies. A major strength of the structural theory is that it provides a cogent account of the motivational systems underlying the dissociative parts, whereby the foundations of mind, behaviour, and personality are affective – motivational in nature. Apparent agency emerges dynamically from these more basic systems, and grounding personality in the action systems and their identifications provides a basis for making sense of both personality differentiation, as well as addressing their origins within a plausible evolutionary framework. As argued earlier, there is no logical difficulty in proposing various drive combinations organised around different apparent centres of agency (self, identity, etc.; cf. Maze, 1983), and if this position is granted, then any "person" is not a substantive entity but rather reflective of a more-or-less stable and ultimately fluid constellation of action systems. Recognising the distinction between self-as-subject and self-as-object thus allows substantiating the knowing subject terms in the action systems, while allowing identity to be potentially fluid. This means that both splits within personality, as well as evolving action system alliances, can give rise to any variety of emerging selves-as-object. Nevertheless, none of the discussion here explicitly addresses how DID arises, such that differing constellations of drives could come to identify with relatively independent senses of self to the exclusion of others. Thus, we need to turn to the process of traumatisation and the division of personality.

Notes

1 For the purposes here, it is sufficient here to treat self and ego as relatively synonymous. See, however, Bertocci (1945) for further discussion about the relation between ego and self.

2 Dalgleish and Power (2004, pp. 813–814), however, point out that Lambie and Marcel (2002) nevertheless at various times treat the "self" as both the subject and object of experience.

3 Such an empirical question is not an easy one to answer, however, since assessing evidence here involves witnessing some complex structure x (for instance) engage in some psychological act y.

4 This is not a fatal criticism since there may be a plausible account for how an object of cognition becomes a knowing subject. For example, in possession cases of DID, some knowing system might assume the "identity" of some type of deity or demon. The point, however, here is that Pica's account is currently incomplete since the subject term is left uncharacterised.

5 Freud's theory of drives (*Triebe*) has a somewhat complicated history, a situation neither helped by *Trieb* being erroneously translated as "Instinct" in the authoritative English translations, and nor by Freud himself. As Pataki (2014a) notes, "drives are inconsistently characterised throughout Freud's work: sometimes as somatic entities, sometimes as psychological entities and sometimes, rather unhelpfully, as borderline entities" (p. 32). See Boag (2017) for further discussion of the concept in Freudian theory.

6 This list is not exclusive and for more recent discussion of primary drives and emotion systems, see Kirsch (2019); Malezieux, Klein, and Gogolla (2023); and Panksepp and Biven (2012).

7 It should be noted that the point here is not to prove any one theory to be correct. Instead, the basic point here is that action systems, so conceived, provide a theoretically sound motivational foundation for human activity, as well as potentially helping to substantiate the elements constituting the smallest knowing units.

8 The structural theory's dualistic division bears an uncanny resemblance to Freud's dualistic division of personality to account for conflict and repression. For instance, Freud initially pitted the self-preservative drives against the sexual ones ("hunger vs love"— Freud, 1910i), before later pitting the life versus death drives, the life drives entailing both self- and species-preservative drives (Freud, 1920g).

9 See also Malezieux, Klein, and Gogolla (2023) for a recent review.

10 As discussed elsewhere (Boag, 2014, 2017), Freud (1910i) similarly refers to the "the collective concept of the 'ego'—a compound which is made up variously at different times" (p. 213). As a "collective" and a "compound", Freud is indicating that the "ego" is not a singular agency or entity, but instead composed of *multiple* motivational sources, and taken as such, the ego is not an irreducible entity but rather a constellation of motivational-action systems of which membership is fluid. Moreover, as Freud often notes, the ego assumes a dominating position within the personality (Freud in Breuer & Freud, 1895d, p. 116; Freud, 1900a, pp. 594–595; 1907a, p. 58), which is a position not inconsistent with the view of the dominance of the ANP in everyday life.

11 This point was not entirely lost on Freud since he was also aware that "the ego can be split; it splits itself during a number of its functions—temporarily at least. Its parts can come together again afterwards" (1933a, p. 58). Freud also recognises that there may be

various possible personality divisions, commenting that "perhaps the secret of the cases of what is described as 'multiple personality' is that the different identifications seize hold of consciousness in turn", a position he describes as not necessarily pathological (1923b, pp. 30–31). Indeed, although the id, ego, and superego are commonly observed personality structures, Freud explicitly writes that variations may nevertheless be found (Freud, 1933a, p. 79).

12 Although the individualism-collectivism distinction might provide broad brushstrokes for characterising culture, it should be kept in mind that any cultural setting is complex and cannot be reduced to such a basic polarity. For an excellent critical discussion of the dichotomy, see Bandura (2002).

Chapter 6

Developmental pathways to structural dissociation

The previous chapter established that there is no logical objection to the possibility of multiple knowers, although accounting for what these knowers are is not straightforward. As discussed, any knower needs to be characterised independently of what it does, and an *in-principle* account needs to be provided of the motivational, affective, and cognitive policies to explain how any such agent or agents act. One strength of the structural theory here is that it provides a coherent foundation for strong partitioning, whereby the action systems constitute the smallest units comprising the "knowers". A further strength is that this approach also offers both an *in-principle* account of their origins, while also addressing their motivational, affective, and cognitive policies. In relation to this, the structural theory of dissociation shares a theoretical affinity with directions in psychodynamic theorising converging on the importance of motivational systems for providing the foundation of personality.

Nonetheless, any such multiplicity of knowers is typically not apparent and, instead, individuals generally view themselves as singular, unified agents (cf. Kihlstrom, 2005). One challenge then is explaining how DID specifically arises, in contrast to the normal development of the self. At first glance, any answer to this question is not likely to be straightforward since the development of DID is said to reflect a complexity of psychological, biological, and environmental causes. Şar et al. (2017), for example, write that "[u]nderstanding the etiology of DID requires integration of trauma exposure, coping, cognitive, neurobiological, systemic, and developmental factors. These include traumatic experiences, family dynamics, child development, and attachment" (p. 143). Be this as it may, extreme stress appears to be the primary factor in disrupting normal personality development, and as developed in Chapter 4, the two major theoretical approaches to explaining structural dissociation are ones based on either Janet's passive-deficit model of dissociation or Freud's active-conflict model entailing repression and defence (Dell, 2009; Gullestad, 2005). The clearest articulation of the Janetian-based approach is found in the structural theory, which proposes that trauma-related dissociation is the result of an integrative deficit (Steele et al., 2014b; Van der Hart et al., 2006). This approach stands in contrast to a psychodynamic approach postulating dissociation as either an active mechanism or outcome of psychological

DOI: 10.4324/9781003328254-6

defence for dealing with traumatisation (e.g., Bromberg 2003; Gullestad, 2005; Schimmenti, 2018).

The aim of this chapter is to consider whether the proposed developmental pathways to DID—deficit and defence—can be coherently formulated. This will be assessed by addressing the postulated mechanisms of the respective theories, and assessing whether these accounts satisfactorily explain a number of relevant phenomena. For instance, if we accept a multiplicity of subject terms, then some account is needed for explaining shifts in executive control, such that one subset of the personality becomes dominant over other parts of the personality (Pataki, 2014b). Additionally, given that some dissociative parts can access certain experiences and others cannot, then some mechanism is required here for explaining how this lack of integration both occurs and is maintained, including the partitioning of thoughts and feelings. These considerations also entail addressing how multiple knowers typically come to identify with a singular self in typical non-dissociative personality development, as well as how this fails to occur in cases such as DID. For the latter, some account is required for potentially explaining how dissociative parts, each with a differing identification of self arise, as well as accounting for how these dissociative parts can, under differing circumstances, know of one another. To achieve this, this chapter focuses on the structural theory given that it champions the clearest articulation of the Janetian passive-deficit account, while also recognising the role of action systems (Van der Hart et al., 2006). After dissecting the claims found within this account, this chapter argues that Janetian-based deficit explanations of dissociation are problematic. Additionally, the proposed role of action systems entails that the structural theory is logically committed to explaining dissociation and DID primarily in terms of a revised psychodynamic theory of defence.

Janetian-based accounts of trauma-dissociation

Rather than addressing how an originally intact personality somehow becomes divided, the structural theory starts with the position that "[a]n integrated personality is a developmental achievement" (Van der Hart et al., 2006, p. 7). As such, the developmental starting point then is a personality system constituted by various action systems that initially lack any coherent personality organisation. Given this starting point, the structural theory needs to explain how normal personality development fails to develop and then how structural dissociation is subsequently maintained. The structural theory's primary explanatory tack here is in line with Janet's account of traumatisation and levels of mental efficiency. As with Janet, these authors write that "[s]tructural dissociation occurs during confrontations with overwhelming events when mental efficiency it too low" (Van der Hart et al., 2006, p. 43). In this sense, integrative deficits arise not primarily due to motivated defence preventing integration (cf. Freud), but rather due to limited mental capacity for dealing with traumatising situations and synthesising experience. This being so, and as with Janet, the structural theory advances a capacity-deficit approach for explaining dissociation, as opposed to dynamic formulations favoured by defence accounts (cf. Dell, 2009).

The specific nature of this deficit is sometimes described as "insufficient psychobiological integration among dissociative parts of the personality" (Steele et al., 2014b, p. 242). Nijenhuis (2019) here rightly observes that this "lack of integration" is what we wish to explain, however, and so any "lack of integration" is not itself an explanation of dissociation. Instead, the structural theory proposes a "capacity" account to address this. As with Janet, structural dissociation results when an event invokes intense emotions and the individual lacks the capacity to integrate these experiences. Van der Hart et al. (2006), for example, write,

> The division of personality constitutes a core feature of trauma. It evolves when the individual lacks the capacity to integrate adverse experiences in part or in full … This division involves two or more insufficiently dynamic but excessively stable subsystems.
>
> (p. 19)

At other times, "deficit" appears to play an explicit causal role given that it is an "ongoing integrative *deficit* that results in a *structural dissociation* of the personality" (Steele et al., 2014b, p. 240, italics in original).

Integrative capacity or deficit is grounded in a Janetian-inspired economy of "mental energy" (see Heim & Bühler, 2019). According to the structural theory here, two interacting factors determine the extent of traumatisation and structural dissociation. One of these is the "objective" characteristics of events, whereby extremely negative, intense, and uncontrollable interpersonal events are likely to be traumatising. The other factor is described in terms of the "subjective characteristics that define the individual's mental energy and mental efficiency (components of integrative capacity)" (Van der Hart et al., 2006, p. 24). Here, Van der Hart et al. follow Janet whereby mental energy is required for maintaining personality integrity after stressful events:

> A high level of mental energy is needed for an individual's personality to remain relatively unified after exposure to extreme stressors. Structural dissociation occurs when an individual's mental efficiency and mental energy … are too low to fully integrate what happened.
>
> (Van der Hart et al., 2006, p. 26; cf. Janet, 1901)

One's "mental level", on the other hand, "indicates the ability to efficiently focus and use whatever mental energy is available in the moment" (Van der Hart et al., 2006, p. 8). This level then determines the individual's mental efficiency and response to the traumatising situation: "Mental efficiency includes the concept of integrative capacity. Thus, being able to reach a high mental level is fundamental to one's capacity to integrate experiences" (Van der Hart et al., 2006, p. 9). Consequently, mental levels are invoked to explain the type of responses people have to traumatising events, such that "[t]he lower their mental level, the more individuals must rely on substitute actions that may protect against overwhelming emotions and thoughts, but that are at odds with integration of traumatic memories and associated dissociative parts" (Van der Hart et al., 2006, p. 12).[1]

Evaluating energy-deficit explanations

It is clearly not unreasonable to say that children may simply be "incapable" of synthesising incompatible facets of psychological experience. For instance, Şar et al. (2017) write that "[o]verwhelmed by intense conflicting needs and emotions, the child is unable to integrate discrete behavioural and emotional states into a coherent or relatively integrated self according to the appropriate sociocultural construction of self" (p. 144). However, so described, this situation appears to reflect a situation of conflict (i.e., contradictory needs), and it is not immediately clear that explanation here is best conceived in terms of a deficit of mental energy. One question then is whether it is even necessary to invoke "mental energy" to explain structural dissociation. The concept of "mental energy" is itself nebulous and there is a long history of criticisms of "mental energy" types of explanation (see Henderson, 1972, for a critical review). Whatever mental energy is, it is generally not equated with "brain energy", the latter fluctuating according to factors such as nutritional intake (Öz et al., 2007).[2] Instead, mental energy concepts are typically metaphors borrowed from physics, and the meaning here is ambiguous as to what such energy might actually be referring to in the context of mind.

One immediate problem following from this is that mental energy is itself both uncharacterised and the only evidence for it, is that which it is meant to explain. This means that the supposed effect is the only evidence of the purported cause: we can only infer if someone has high mental level when a person is mentally healthy and integrated, or infer whether someone has low mental energy based on some state, such as structural dissociation. If it is the case that there is no independent evidence for such mental energy apart from what it is said to explain, then we are left then with a form of circularity: what causes the person to be mentally healthy and integrated? The person's high mental energy and efficiency. And how do we know that the person has high mental energy and efficiency? The person is mentally healthy and integrated. And what causes the person to be mentally healthy and integrated? And so on. Consequently, energy accounts are both ontologically obscure and *prima facie* fail as explanatory mechanisms.[3]

Of course, one might retort here that although we cannot presently say what this energy precisely is, it may nevertheless be discovered in the future. There is also no theoretical problem with explaining events via unseen causes. After all, as Hopkins (1988) notes, any account of behaviour typically invokes "unseen" processes (such as motives and beliefs), which we typically infer on the basis of effects (i.e., sequences of apparently motivated movements) (p. 38).[4] Moreover, physics invokes presently unobservable processes or entities based on manifested effects: "the physicist surmises the existence of electrical particles of atoms by the effects they produce" (Beres, 1962, p. 309). That being said, energy types of explanations are nevertheless logically unsuitable explanatory terms since they are essentially redescriptions of that which they should explain (at least in their present form). As indicated above, without being able to say what this energy is, independent of what it should explain, then we have circular explanation (the *explanans* and *explanandum* are not logically distinct from one another). Consider, for instance, the claim that "[m]ental efficiency includes the concept of integrative capacity. Thus being able to reach a high mental level is fundamental to one's capacity to integrate experiences" (Van der Hart et al., 2006, p. 9). Using "integrative capacity" here to explain personality integration is problematic because without some independent sense of what this capacity might actually be, any "integrative capacity" essentially refers to whether someone is able to integrate their personality or not. Since whether someone is able to integrate their personality or not is the *effect* that we are attempting to explain, capacity accounts are problematic since they confuse causes with effects. In a similar fashion, terms such as "deficit" are similarly descriptive, so the earlier statement "ongoing integrative *deficit* that results in a *structural dissociation* of the personality" (Steele et al., 2014b, p. 240, italics in original) is circular since "the deficit" is essentially a redescription of "structural dissociation".

The problem above for the structural theory is not helped by invoking "causal powers", as seen in Nijenhuis's (2019) attempt to salvage capacity accounts in terms of "manifest reciprocal powers" (p. 85). Such causal powers are typically framed in terms of X having the power to bring about Y, and, for this reason, any such "power" is again simply a description of what something can do (*viz.* the power to bring about the effect). "Powers" thus cannot stand as coherent explanatory terms since they are conceptually bound to what they are said to explain (see Passmore, 1935). Moreover, invoking teleology simply compounds the problem (e.g., powers being a "longing" or "a striving [manifest power] to realize" certain aims—Nijenhuis, 2019, p. 86) because goals or ends are similarly what require explanation.[5]

None of this is to deny, however, that background variables such as psychological immaturity (or fatigue, or sleep deprivation, etc.) might be implicated as causal factors relevant to understanding structural dissociation. In fact, if all that is meant by "deficit" is that the individual lacks certain skills or attributes necessary for adequately dealing with circumstances, then there is no necessary logical problem with this. For example, a young child's brain structures may simply be at a stage where personality integration is still incomplete, which, then, in interaction with social circumstances, leads to structural dissociation:

> Structural dissociation involves hindrance or breakdown of a natural progression toward integration of psychobiological systems of the personality... It involves a *chronic* integrative deficit largely due to a combination of the child's immature integrative brain structures and functions... and inadequate psychophysiological regulation by caregivers, such as insufficient soothing, calming, and modulation.
>
> (Van der Hart et al., 2006, p. 7, italics in original)

In the example above, brain structures, social factors, and structural dissociation are logically independent from one another, and so can stand in causal relationship to one another. This being so, if an "integrative deficit" refers to factors such as psychological immaturity, then there is potentially no problem with such immaturity standing as a causal factor, presuming that the *explanans* and *explanandum* can be cast in logically distinct terms.[6]

The vulnerability of childhood

One background factor relevant to DID is the developmental epoch of early childhood, with "childhood attachment-based trauma appearing to be a universal factor" (Dorahy et al., 2014, p. 412). There are, of course, various grounds for why children may be particularly vulnerable to traumatisation and structural dissociation. This life period constitutes a sensitive period of rapid brain development, and the developing brain here appears particularly sensitive to extreme stress that can result in lasting brain modifications (Andersen et al., 2008; Nemeroff, 2016; Schore, 2002). Childhood is also a sensitive period for personality development based on attachment needs interacting with socio-contextual factors (Blizard, 2003; Bowlby, 1969). Children require an emotionally supportive environment to meet attachment needs, while typically also lacking skills for successfully coping with highly stressful events (Van der Hart et al., 2006). Moreover, as proponents of the structural theory observe, unlike ordinary adults who have more or less developed a coherent and stable identity, children are far more vulnerable with respect to their developing personalities:

> Because young children have not developed a coherent personality structure, they are especially susceptible to trauma. Abuse and neglect can alter the mind and the brain of young children in ways that promote state-dependent or personality-dependent functioning. Their rudimentary behavioral states (that are shaped by different action systems) can become easily dissociated.
>
> (Steele et al., 2014b, p. 245)

Thus, the developmental context of family dynamics and attachment needs contribute to the causal field for structural dissociation. What the above also demonstrates is that terms such as "capacity", "deficit", or "mental level" are, at best, placeholders for more specific explanatory factors. Consequently, once the relevant causal field factors are identified, then there is simply no need for capacity or mental economic types of accounts.

Is defence relevant to explaining structural dissociation?

The redundancy of using deficit as an explanation is further seen in examples where defence appears to be clearly implicated in accounts of structural dissociation. Consider, for instance, the example from holocaust survivor Aharon Appelfeld on recounting traumatic memories. He writes that "*[t]he moment any memory or shred of a memory was about to float upwards, we would fight against it as though against evil spirits*" (cited in Van der Hart et al., 2006, p. 53, italics in original). Appelfeld's description here would appear to suggest, if anything, that dissociation is at least maintained via motivated rejection of painful memories (i.e., defence). Van der Hart et al., however, comment here that "[t]his example demonstrates that without sufficient mental efficiency, traumatized individuals may find the past too painful to integrate, so that they continue to respond to potent reminders of traumatic experiences with alarm or other defensive reactions" (p. 53). Nevertheless, given that we have no evidence of mental energy or "mental efficiency" independent of such reactions, the example cannot be said to provide evidence for insufficient mental efficiency. If anything, citing insufficient mental efficiency appears redundant because the situation can be both more parsimoniously and sufficiently cast in terms of defence against overwhelming affects (and/or lack of alternative coping skills).

The example from Appelfeld above is not an isolated one, and there are other examples that would indicate that psychological defence might be relevant to explaining dissociation. For instance, Van der Hart et al. open their 2006 book on structural dissociation with a quote from the former Miss America and incest survivor Marilyn Van Derbur, who writes, *"[w]ithout realizing it, I fought to keep my two worlds separated. Without ever knowing why, I made sure, whenever possible, that nothing passed between the compartmentalization I had created between the day child and the night child"* (in Van der Hart et al., 2006, p. 1, italics in original). "Fighting to keep worlds separate" is clearly a motivated defensive activity, and although explaining how such defence operates presents theoretical challenges (see Chapter 4), the example again suggests that defence rather than deficit is both implicated and perhaps sufficient for explaining aspects of structural dissociation.

Proponents of the structural theory do, of course, acknowledge that defence is relevant to understanding the role of EPs. Steele et al. (2014b), for example, write that "[p]sychological defense is compatible with our proposal that dissociation is grounded in specific action systems, including those of physical defense" (p. 244). Nevertheless, these authors believe that such psychological defences are a *secondary* occurrence following after the initial structural deficit: "Although dissociation is viewed [by others] as a primary psychological defense, we contend that that psychological defense occurs secondarily to the deficit in integrative capacity (at least initially)" (Steele et al., 2014b, pp. 244–245). Van der Hart et al. (2006) similarly write that it is the deficit that occurs first, which may then later become a defence: "structural dissociation begins as a deficit during traumatization, but can become a mental defense and a way of coping with the mere unpleasantness of life" (pp. 75-76). This causal relationship then is that structural dissociation first arises due to a deficit (i.e., deficit is necessary for causing dissociation), whereas defence might occur as a secondary coping response.

As already discussed above, deficit accounts are problematic, and one of the biggest arguments for defence playing a primary role in structural dissociation is that dissociative symptoms are themselves outcomes of *defensive responses.* Defensive responses here can be seen as animal (including human) psychological and behavioural responses against threatening and painful events. In this respect, Nijenhuis, Vanderlinden, and Spinhoven (1998) draw "a phylogenetic parallel … between characteristic dissociative responses and behavioral and physiological animal defensive and recuperative states" (p. 254; cf. Putnam, 1992). Such defensive responses are innate and so automatic (i.e., unlearnt) and are comprehensible within an evolutionary context, whereby animals (including humans) must rapidly deal with threats to survival. Given that dissociative responses are postulated to be associated with defensive responses, and extreme stress and threat are causally relevant to explaining structural dissociation, then such defences would be expected to occur both automatically and immediately as the *primary* response threat. This means then that defence arising from extreme threat is better placed to explain structural dissociation than invoking "mental energy" or "deficit", these latter terms, if anything, simply providing broad labels describing the context of childhood. Defence thus appears to be the primary factor for understanding how structural dissociation emerges when children are faced with extreme threat and stress. What the above further indicates is that the structural theory of dissociation cannot both say that dissociative responses are innate defensive reactions to threat and then also posit that defence occurs *after* "an integrative deficit". Instead, the temporal arrangement appears to be that threat is perceived first, which triggers a subsequent defensive response, the latter somehow leading to structural dissociation. There is subsequently no justification in invoking mental energy, integrative capacity, or deficit as the primary cause of structural dissociation. Consequently, a primary role for defence in structural dissociation emerges within the structural theory itself.

Assessing defence explanations for structural dissociation

As already developed in Chapter 4, defence is commonly addressed in teleological terms such that defensive dissociation occurs *in order to* protect against distress or being overwhelmed (e.g., Bromberg, 2003). However, if defence does play a role, then it is not a teleological one, and so any plausible account of defence needs to be explained non-teleologically (i.e., in terms of efficient causes). With respect to this, there are existing accounts of defence that can be formulated non-teleologically. For example, as discussed in Chapter 4, Purcell (2019) views dissociation as "a protective *reaction* that occurs *reflexively* in traumatic experience" (p. 318, italics in original). In this sense, Purcell compares dissociation to a fight or flight response, something then which is reflexive and automatic but not something intended (i.e., not based on desire and guided by belief). He writes, "dissociation in response to trauma is *entirely automatic*-purposeful but *not* intentional, consciously or unconsciously" (p. 318, italics in original). This can be taken to mean that dissociation is a reflexive response triggered in response to threat (in the same way as one might pull one's hand away from a hot stove). Cognition is, nevertheless, still implicated since any fight-or-flight response requires awareness co-ordinated with the invoking situational event (e.g., to avoid the source of threat). Consequently, any such defence cannot be reduced to a non-cognitive reflex that precludes awareness of threat. Be this as it may, and as developed in Chapter 2, such threat detection can nevertheless occur unconsciously since it is possible to take x to be a threat without knowing that x is perceived as threatening. As such, and within the context of the structural theory (Van der Hart et al., 2006), any given action system could potentially know and respond to a threat, without either knowing this itself, or any other action system knowing of this situation. There is thus merit to Purcell's position, but the implications require fleshing out[7], and some plausible mechanism for explaining dissociative defence is still required.

A potential mechanism for structural dissociation and non-teleological defence

One potential explanatory avenue here emerges from Şar et al.'s (2017) earlier observation that conflict is relevant to explaining structural dissociation. Such conflict is broadly recognised throughout diverse areas of psychology (e.g., as with approach-avoidance conflict—Carver, 2006; Elliot, 2006), as well as providing the platform for the psychoanalytic account of mind (Freud, 1915c, 1915d). On this viewpoint, humans and other species accommodate a variety of motivational states, some of which may cooperate or conflict with another. In the latter instance, one's desires may conflict with one's moral beliefs, awareness of which leads to distress and "mental torment" (Freud in Breuer & Freud, 1895d, p. 165). In a non-teleological psychodynamic view, defence might thereafter follow as a response to the negative affective state, rather than in terms of protecting the mind from conflict.

Motivational conflict is also apparent in the structural theory of dissociation, whereby personality integration involves integrating and balancing out motivational systems with competing agendas. Van der Hart et al (2006), for instance, write that "individuals must integrate action systems, which can be a daunting task because combining action systems is more challenging than engaging in a single one. Indeed, many common psychological conflicts involve difficulty in balancing such different interests" (Van der Hart et al., 2006, pp. 32–33). The structural theory thus views the mind as an economy of potentially competing demands, and such motivational conflict would consequently appear to be a possible source of any failure of integration. The structural theory is actually particularly well placed to accommodate conflict, since, as noted in the previous chapter, the structural theory accepts a taxonomy of basic emotions (Panksepp & Biven, 2012), as well as proposing a basic dualism that addresses the protagonists involved in conflict. As Van der Hart et al. (2006) write, "dissociative divisions... primarily take place between the two major categories of psychobiological systems that make up personality" (p. 3). As discussed in the previous chapter, these two broad categories of action systems are the systems related to sustaining life, relations, and reproduction ("adapting to daily life"), on the one hand, and "those that serve survival of the individual by promoting defense in the face of threat" (Steele et al., 2014b, p. 243).[8]

Attachment and approach-avoidance conflict

As mentioned in the previous chapter, the structural theory's dualistic division here also bears some resemblance to Freud's initial dualistic division of personality to account for conflict, whereby the self-preservative drives are pitted against the sexual ones (what Freud described in shorthand as "hunger vs love"—Freud, 1910i).[9] Freud, however, noted that there was no theoretical objection to other sources of conflict (Freud, 1940a), and one potential candidate for motivational conflict during childhood that appears relevant for explaining structural dissociation concerns attachment needs. According to attachment theory (Bowlby, 1969, 1973, 1980), children are hardwired to turn to caregivers for comfort and security when threatened. When the caregiver is also the source of threat, an insoluble conflict situation is created (Holmes, 2003). As Blizard (2003) notes, this "double bind" situation "places the child in an irresolvable paradox; wherein she can neither approach the caregiver, flee, nor shift attention to the environment" (p. 33). This is essentially an extreme approach-avoidance conflict situation that could provide a potential developmental context for the development of DID (Blizard, 2003; Liotti, 2004; Şar et al., 2017). Various theorists, in fact, propose that such incompatible interactions with caregivers could feasibly lead to dissociated personality parts. Blizard (2003), for instance, notes, that "[t]he child's rapid alternation between approach and avoidance strategies may develop into incompatible, segregated systems of attachment, which could become dissociated executors or self states, the basis of DID" (p. 35).[10] Such approach-avoidance conflict may be further evident in disorganised/disoriented (Type D) attachment, whereby the contradictory interactions with caregivers lead children to display contradictory behaviour patterns based upon incoherent working models (Main & Solomon, 1986). In this respect, Steele et al. (2014b) propose that this situation could help explain structural dissociation:

> ... Type D attachment involves concurrent or rapid successive activations of the attachment system and the defense action system in a child who simultaneously approaches and defends against a scary caregiver. This insoluble approach-avoidance dilemma can promote a structural dissociation of the attachment system and the defensive system that generates an ANP and an EP.
> (p. 245)

Whether disorganised attachment is necessary or not for DID is an empirical question, but such attachment is certainly associated with DID (Dorahy et al., 2014) and consistent with a developmental context ripe for structural dissociation to develop based on irresolvable conflict. This indicates that both traumatisation and conflict models can work together, whereby extreme threat activates competing systems with incompatible aims, that then leads to the unintended consequence of structural dissociation.

Inhibition as a potential explanatory mechanism

The discussion above indicates that there is a plausible context for the development of psychological conflict and incompatible responses leading to structural dissociation. However, a mechanism is still required for explaining how traumatisation-conflict leads to structural dissociation specifically, instead of a single apparent agent comprehending incompatible desires and needs (cf. Nijenhuis, 2015). A plausible mechanism is also required for explaining how structural dissociation and DID arise and function such that different dissociate personality parts can take executive control to the exclusion of others.

One candidate mechanism that might help to explain structural dissociation involves inhibitory mechanisms, which restrain certain actions from occurring. The need for inhibitory processes is generally well recognised since some account is required for explaining how "conflicting response tendencies" (Ridderinkhof et al., 2004, p. 129) or "competition between incompatible inputs" (Redgrave et al., 1999, p. 1016) (i.e., conflicting motives) are resolved so to allow some actions to be executed and others prevented. For example, changes in environmental circumstances might demand that one response (e.g., eating) be rapidly terminated to allow another response to occur (e.g., fleeing) (Branco & Redgrave, 2020). Although the specific neural bases of inhibitory mechanisms are still not well established (Stuphorn, 2015), there can be no doubt that such mechanisms both exist and are necessary for explaining behaviour generally. The simple reason for this is that for any prioritised action to occur, competing actions must also be restrained and prevented from interfering with the action's execution. Put differently, when there are two competing courses of action, X and Y, for X to occur both X must be activated while Y must be inhibited and prevented from accessing the relevant motor execution systems (although not necessarily prevented from non-relevant ones) (Redgrave et al., 1999). Diamond et al. (1963), in fact, early on recognise that a complex organism with multiple action potentialities requires some type of inhibitory mechanism for efficient action to happen. As these authors note, should responses be merely antagonistic, then any behavioural output is likely to be ineffective for responding to the situation since it could reflect an uncoordinated mixture of responses interfering with one another. As such, coordinated movement requires a mechanism of restraint and inhibition of interfering responses:

> One very important function of a nervous apparatus is to provide an arrangement whereby, when the same organism has multiple response potentialities, one of these can be activated without simultaneously activating the others. If the several response systems are to be coordinated, and not independent, inhibition is required.
>
> (Diamond et al., 1963, p. 69)

Postulating some type of inhibitory mechanism is also more or less already present within the structural theory. Nijenhuis et al. (1998), for instance, note that defensive responses are mutually inhibitive (e.g., aggressive responding inhibits affiliative ones), where, for example, the action systems mediating ANPs and EPs tend to inhibit one another. Steele et al. (2014b), in a like manner, write that "[u] nder threat, action systems of daily life will be inhibited; in the absence of threat, defense systems will be inhibited" (p. 243). Van der Hart et al. (2006) similarly write that

> [w]hen an individual has structural dissociation, a dissociative part of the personality will be directed by the particular goals of the action systems that motivate that part, and will inhibit or avoid other goals related to action systems that are dissociated in other parts of the personality.
>
> (p. 33).

Inhibition is also invoked to address *switching* of executive control, where, for instance, Steele et al. (2014b) write that "[i]n children who are structurally dissociated, this defensive response will include reactivation of the EP and an inhibition of the ANP" (p. 246).

Any adequate account of inhibition needs, however, to be more than a redescription of "preventing a response from occurring" so as to avoid circularity. Inhibition also needs to be addressed without reference to some type of an executive acting to resolve incompatible inputs. As developed in the previous chapter, there is no justification for postulating such an over-arching self-system with its own motivational policies to stand over and above the other motivational systems. The problem with any such perspective is apparent in Brown's (2006) cognitive model of DID. Brown proposes that traumatising environments might first set up incompatible behavioural goals (e.g., approach-avoidance), whereby a cognitive system then works to manage anxiety by acting "to prevent the simultaneous activation of the conflicting goals" (p. 23). Hypotheses are subsequently made concerning the conflicting inputs, which are then "repeatedly sampled by a primary attentional system (PAS), which selects one of the hypotheses as the most appropriate account of the current situation" (p. 17). To explain inhibition, Brown proposes that a "secondary attentional system (SAS)" "may intervene to bias the activation levels of relevant programs" in situations where the primary attentional system cannot produce adaptive responses (e.g., novel situations) (p. 18). This secondary system acts here then as a "supervisory attentional system" that employs problem-solving algorithms to enact intentions: "Processing controlled by the SAS is *willed*..., effortful. deliberate and associated with a subjective character of self-awareness (i.e., an awareness of being aware) labelled *secondary awareness*" (Brown, 2011, p. 218, italics in original). This SAS is presumably the self-as-agent or ego, and as with any such agency, it must presumably then have its own set of motives to explain selection and inhibition. Again, what these motivational policies might actually be is unclear, and given that the only evidence for such systems is in terms of what they are intended to explain, these appear to be nothing more than reified homunculi that cannot coherently explain inhibition.

Avoiding circular explanation requires that the explanans be logically independent of the effects to be explained (the explanandum). Consequently, any process of inhibition requires formulation in terms of the respective components and interactions, independently of the effects that inhibition is said to explain. One starting point is to first address the protagonists underlying conflict and inhibition. As developed in the previous chapter, the action systems are well placed here since they can be substantiated as subject terms that both guide cognition and play an inhibitory role. In relation to this, Van der Hart et al. (2006), for example, observe that "subsystems restrict an individual's field of consciousness to relevant stimuli (e.g., particular aspects of eating, safety, relationship, work) and promote certain action tendencies, *while inhibiting others*" (p. 33, italics added). Moreover, there are normally degrees of "reciprocal inhibition", such as with attachment and defence systems inhibiting one another (Van der Hart et al., 2006). Proposing that action systems play an inhibitory role obviates any discussion of identifying some type of inhibiting or censoring agency (see Boag, 2017; Maze & Henry, 1996). Instead, it is the action systems that underlie motivational conflict, and that sometimes work together or cancel one another out depending upon circumstances. Nevertheless, the term "inhibition" is still descriptive and we still need to address not only how one set of action systems underlying a dissociative part becomes active, while somehow preventing other sets of action systems from accessing executive control.

Competing interests and the winner-takes-all model

Substantiating inhibition in any theoretical sense requires postulating a clear mechanism of how traumatising experiences specifically interfere with personality development and how structural dissociation is developed and maintained. One possible conceptual model that could address both structural dissociation and switches of executive control is a winner-takes-all neural model for understanding both normal and pathological behaviour. Such a model operates via competing inputs, thresholds, and shut-off mechanisms (Redgrave et al., 1999; cf. Boag, 2017). This mechanism has been postulated with respect to the "selection problem" described earlier (*viz.* competing responses and response selection). The neural mechanism works along the following lines: when there are competing motivational inputs, any given behavioural outcome results from one input reaching a threshold that shuts off competing inputs and allows execution of the action. It appears clear that certain motivational states have priority over others according to specific circumstances (e.g., foraging behaviour will be terminated in the presence of threat; Choi et al., 2022). Such prioritisation is presumably a function of relevant deprivation and urgency (what is typically described as the "salience" of the reward or threat). For example, daily life activities such as "eating" could be expected to occur when both "hunger" is somatically activated and food available, while in the absence of immediate threat. However, should a threat arise, responding to the threat could be expected to take priority over eating, causing the termination of eating behaviour and the activation of fleeing behaviour (i.e., a switching of behaviour).

The above example demonstrates that a winner-takes-all neural model could account for the inhibition of dissociative parts, whereby the urgent affective demands of one action system could prevent other action systems from having access to both psychological and behavioural systems (see Boag, 2017). In the context of childhood traumatisation, intense fear could trigger the winner-takes-all threshold, whereby the activation of defence systems precludes other action systems from accessing the relevant motor systems and attendant knowledge (see also here Song, Lin and Liu (2023)). Developmentally, growing up under relatively normal circumstances would allow children to integrate both daily life and defence action systems into a relatively coherent pattern of engagements with the world, whereby the individual regularly engages in both sets of activities, allowing a relatively coherent self-image to develop that embraces both sets of motivational systems (e.g., I am someone who is sometimes happy, but also someone who is sometimes angry). However, in unpredictable and highly threatening situations, there is presumably less opportunity for daily life and defence systems to act in any co-ordinated fashion, and so less opportunity for a coherent self to develop. As in animal settings, if an animal is eating and then suddenly a predator appears, eating needs to be shut down immediately to allow escape or some other defensive act to occur[11]. If a child is exposed to unpredictable threats, then the shutting down of daily life systems would be an extreme but necessary response (cf. Nijenhuis et al., 1998), potentially leading to daily life and defence become mutually exclusive sets of systems. Such a context would provide a basis for the development of separate identities revolving around the differing sets of action systems, as well as addressing how intense affective states such as fear and anger trigger changes of executive control.

The theoretical position above is consistent with the structural theory, whereby inhibition and dissociation in the context of the structural theory could first arise when traumatic stress leads to defence systems inhibiting daily life systems, resulting in the "natural fault line" observed in structural dissociation (Steele et al., 2014b; Van der Hart et al., 2006). Such inhibition also lays claim to being the primary explanation of structural dissociation:

[w]hen there is trauma-related structural dissociation of the personality, the coordination and coherence of action systems seems to be disrupted. Because action systems of daily life and action systems of defense naturally inhibit one another, traumatic stress will more readily derail their mutual *integration*.

(Steele et al., 2014b, p. 244, italics in original)

Accordingly, given that such inhibition and resulting dissociation is threat based, we essentially have a "threat-inhibition-dissociation" explanation of structural dissociation: "We thus propose that a threat-driven dissociative division between action systems of daily life and action systems of defense substantially accounts for the prototypical organizations of ANPs and EPs" (Steele et al., 2014b, p. 244). If this is the case, then we have a non-teleological psychodynamic position, whereby conflict between behavioural systems explains how "trauma" interferes with personality development leading to structural dissociation. There is thus no need to posit any type of deficit as playing a primary causal role.

Nevertheless, one potential theoretical hurdle here concerns the claim that EPs can have an ongoing sense of real and immediate danger, experiencing the traumatising events as if it were currently occurring (cf. Van der Hart, et al., 2006). On the proposal above, one might expect that EPs would then dominate executive control all of the time given the presumed priority of fear over other motivational states.[12] This is a very important consideration, and by way of response, psychodynamic thinking also generally recognises that individuals can have ongoing experiences of intense affective states that can both exist unconsciously and without directly impacting upon behaviour. For instance, with Freudian repression, the repressed remains explicitly intense, despite remaining unconscious: "The mark of something repressed is precisely that in spite of its intensity it is unable to enter consciousness" (Freud, 1907a, p. 48). Addressing then how EPs can experience a sense of ongoing danger but without necessarily taking control is likely then best explained in terms of the ANP's response to perceiving EPs as threats. According to the structural theory, ANPs phobically avoid intrusions of EPs, which itself helps maintain structural dissociation. Van der Hart et al. (2006), for instance, write: "Structural dissociation is specifically maintained when ANPs learn to phobically and chronically avoid intruding EPs with their traumatic memories and accompanying aversive sensations, emotions, and thoughts" (p. 13). Such motivated avoidance is essentially a form of psychological conflict, triggered by intense fear or other aversive emotional responses. As these same authors write: "The phobia of trauma-derived mental actions evolves from the core phobia of traumatic memories, and involves the survivor's fear, disgust, or shame about mental actions he or she has associated with traumatic memories. As long as patients are afraid of their inner life, they cannot integrate their internal experiences, so that structural dissociation is ongoing" (Van der Hart et al., 2006, p. 14). This means that the ANP's awareness of threat and ongoing fear could act as factors that prevents the EP from having greater control. Such a situation is essentially then the same as what is postulated in Freudian repression, whereby the ego knows the threat to maintain repression but is prevented from *knowing (or acknowledging) that the threat is known* (see Boag, 2012 for further discussion).[13]

Be this as it may, although threat-defence-inhibition appears to provide a primary causal explanation of structural dissociation (within the structural theory itself), this is not to say that factors such as fatigue and psychological immaturity are irrelevant. Such factors are presumably background components constituting the causal field. In the context of childhood, normal development typically involves the gradual organisation and synthesis of these action systems working together in a more or less coherent and co-ordinated fashion, which then allows the action systems to more or less identify with a singular sense of self. However, given that there are multiple action systems, there is no guarantee that any such co-ordinated synthesis will occur, and more or less pathological personality development involves a failure of this integration. As Steele et al. (2014b) observe: "Young children are still developing a coherent personality organization. Thus, the earliest developmental pathways to structural dissociation of the personality probably involve hindering the natural integration of action systems and 'discrete behavioural states'" (p. 245; cf. Van der Hart et al., 2006). Nevertheless, acknowledging that variables such as psychological maturity and fatigue are implicated does not mean endorsing explanations in terms of "mental levels" because such descriptions are, at best, simply a placeholder for other such specific factors.

Addressing the integration of dissociative parts

A remaining issue is accounting for how any dissociative part could more or less suddenly emerge or disappear, and how multiple parts can manage to then fuse with one another into a single identity. As Van der Hart et al. (2006) note, "[d]issociative parts maintain particular psychobiological boundaries that keep them divided, but they can in principle dissolve" (p. 19). On the position developed above, given the postulated role of defence for explaining dissociation, working through traumatisation would be necessary for integration. The structural theory similarly postulates that working through traumatisation provides grounds for integration: "ANP and EP eventually must be integrated into a unified personality so that ANP realizes what has happened, and EP realizes traumatizing events have ended" (Van der Hart et al., 2006, p. 57). In this respect, phasic approaches to therapy for DID appear to provide opportunities for re-evaluating threats by establishing a sense of safety and working through memories of traumatising events (International Society for the Study of Trauma and Dissociation, 2011). What presumably occurs then is that the boundaries between sets of subsystems are no longer maintained by defence. Shifts in identity could then feasibly occur in response to reorganising the constellations of action systems. As discussed in the previous chapter, the action systems are well placed to substantiate the knowing systems, which, however, do not know themselves directly. What is known, if anything, is the self-as-object (typically taken to be some type of self-image or self-representation), and it is this self-as-object that is amenable to change. Thus, what may initially be two sets of action systems with independent selves might come to be co-ordinated with one another, cohering more or less around a singular self. In such cases, daily life systems could come to act with defence systems, allowing the possibility of the two sets of systems to develop a relatively unified sense of the individual in relation to the world.

Summary

The Janetian contribution to explaining DID is problematic since invoking "mental energy" and mental levels as explanatory variables raises issues of circularity and redundancy. However, an alternative non-teleological account of defence also emerges within the structural theory and appears to be the primary explanatory factor for understanding structural dissociation. Here, the developmental context of childhood and attachment needs leads to an opportunity for an irresolvable conflict when the child is faced with extreme threat within a caregiver context. This sets up a context of mutually exclusive responses, which, within the developmental context, leads to structural dissociation. One possible explanatory mechanism mediating this outcome entails inhibitory neural processes, which contribute to a relatively permanent separation of the action systems. Nevertheless, relearning experiences afford opportunities for development and integration of the formerly competing motivational trends.

Notes

1 Mental levels can also be a lasting *effect* of traumatisation. Van der Hart et al. (2006) on this point note that "[m]any survivors have difficulty attaining and sustaining higher mental levels, regardless of how much mental energy is available to them" (p. 8). Dissociation may then be maintained by individuals with insufficient mental level being unable to effectively meet life's challenges: "Inadequate mental actions are also implicit in the ongoing maintenance of dissociation. Such actions are referred to as *substitute actions*, those that are less adaptive than required when the challenges of life exceed the mental level of the patient" (Van der Hart et al., 2006, p. 10, italics in original).

2 The concept of "brain energy" within nutrition research also appears not without controversy, with motivation appearing to be the major underlying concept of energy formulations (see Barbuto and Jnr, 2006; O'Conner, 2006).

3 Freud's "economic" view of the mind, which also invokes mental energy, is similarly problematic (see Boag, 2017 for further critical discussion).

4 See, however, Maze (1983) and Michell (1988) for the claim that we can and do, in some instances, observe cognition in action.

5 Again, humans do appear to act in a goal-directed manner, and so any explanation of human activity needs to satisfactorily address this. However, and as developed earlier, any explanation must be consistent with efficient causality entailing mechanism and causal antecedents, rather than ends. Efficient causality need not deny a role for human consciousness (e.g., fore-thought, planning), however, since such mental activities can operate as causal antecedents underlying apparent goal-directed activity (Maze, 1983). As such, the apparent teleology associated with "reasons" (versus causes) can be accommodated within a natural science framework embracing efficient causality (see Boag, 2017).

6 There is also, of course, no necessary problem with the claim that certain events and deprivations during early developmental periods may leave behind profound deficits that may further constitute factors maintaining structural dissociation (e.g., failing to learn affect regulation due to inadequate mirroring and containment—Fonagy et al., 2004).

7 Purcell (2019), however, also takes dissociation to entail "unformulated experience", a position currently popular in psychodynamic theorising. On this account, some psychological experiences exist in non-representable and nondeclarative form (e.g., experiences before the onset of infantile amnesia). For critical discussion of this in the context of defence, see Boag (2020).

8 A discussed below, motivated conflict is also implicated in the role of phobic avoidance for maintaining structural dissociation.

9 Freud, of course, later contrasted the life versus death drives (Freud, 1920g), but these "drives" are without clear motivating structures and described teleologically, and so not the account accepted here.

10 As will be discussed below, Blizard (2003) proposes a teleological defence account for explaining how the dissociation specifically occurs.
11 See Misslin (2003) for discussion of the distinction between anticipatory and immediate defence behaviour.
12 I thank Martin Dorahy for this important observation.
13 Van der Hart et al. (2006) also recognise that EPs "are often mediated by only one action system or a limited constellation of action systems" (p. 210) and so one further possible explanation for why EPs do not generally dominate is that motivational reinforcement is required from non-EP relevant action systems (e.g., recognition of some actual threat by the ANP).

Conclusion and going forward

This work set out to address whether trauma-dissociation and DID could be coherently formulated and to address the theoretical status of dissociative parts with respect to personality and identity. To achieve this, conceptual and theoretical analysis within a realist theoretical framework was employed, with a particular focus upon the concept of relation. Conceptual and theoretical research was deemed necessary since the crux of the controversy here appears to be conceptual in nature. As both advocates and critics alike recognise, conceptual and theoretical confusion pervades the topic of dissociation and DID (Kihlstrom, 2005; Nijenhuis & Van der Hart, 2011; Van der Hart et al., 2004; Van der Hart & Dorahy, 2023). In relation to this, conceptual clarity is needed to assess what is precisely meant by trauma-dissociation since trauma can refer to either an event, an experience, or an effect (Weathers & Keane, 2008; Zepf & Zepf, 2008). Similarly, dissociation is sometimes taken to describe a psychological process, structure, defence, deficit, or symptom (cf. Cardeña & Gleaves, 2007). On the other hand, any debate concerning whether dissociative parts are personalities or not is not likely to be productive if we fail to have a clear understanding of personality, identity, and self.

The foregoing analysis establishes that it is possible to coherently formulate the development of structural dissociation entailing strong partitioning using a revised model of defence. As developed in the preceding chapters, the action systems provide a coherent foundation for motivation, cognition, and affective processes, along with constituting the smallest knowing units within the organism. Given that the mind appears initially as a plurality of potentially competing interests, the development of a more or less coherent self is a developmental achievement. Attachment-relevant contexts, where caregivers are both sources of security and threat, appear to provide the conditions ripe for preventing the development of a singular self. Motivational conflict forces the action systems to instead cohere around their independent competing interests and identify with their limited ranges of experiences. Given that any personality or self is more or less a dominant set of action systems, dissociative parts each have as much claim to being personalities as any other "normal" one.

The position above thus has far-reaching implications for understanding normal personality. As others recognise, the study of dissociation affords an

DOI: 10.4324/9781003328254-7

opportunity to address both normal and disordered personality and what it means to be a person, generally. On this point, Cardeña (1994), comments: "Ironically, perhaps one of the great appeals of the domain of dissociation is that it allows the investigator and the clinician to connect various areas within psychology (e.g., personality, memory, consciousness, identity) that up until recently have been dissociated" (p. 27). In this respect, Manning and Manning (2007) aptly underscore the valuable insight gained from the study of traumatisation and the impact upon the developing mind for understanding the normal psyche. Underlying the apparent unity of the so-called normal personality is an economy of competing interests that can come to both cohere and conflict with one another. If so, then these subpersonal motivational systems, shaped by the cultural milieu, constitute the foundations of who we are as persons. What we take to be a "person" then is simply an appearance that belies the primitive motivational systems that provide the foundations of mind.

It needs to be kept clearly in mind, however, that the aim of work is not to prove whether trauma-dissociation and DID are real occurrences or not. Conceptual and theoretical work such as this can only point to possible conceptual problems associated with various positions and propose theoretical pathways to avoid those same problems. In this respect, this work identifies conceptual problems associated with both the Janetian- and Freudian-derived accounts of dissociation. Nevertheless, a coherent and plausible account of traumatisation and conflict for making sense of trauma-dissociation and DID is possible. Of course, this work might be taken to simply reflect "theoretical speculation". However, both the empirical evidence for action systems, along with arguments against postulating any such self-as-agent somehow standing independently of these motivational sources, means that the common-sense view of self is problematic. Moreover, the clear convergence upon affective neuroscience by both Janetian and psychodynamic perspectives points to the value of a revised psychodynamic view for providing a basic model for understanding personality and its disorders generally.

Going forward

Going forward requires much more than theory, however, and there are a number of barriers here to convincingly demonstrating the thesis outlined above. As previously discussed, traumatisation involves a complex process entailing both psychobiological and socio-cultural variables. For that reason, both the components of personality, along with addressing the complex interaction between persons and situations, require consideration. Consequently, sufficiently addressing the role of traumatic stress on personality development requires a position that integrates the complexity of situations, as well as being consistent with a deterministic psychology that extends beyond simple cause-effect relations to address complex change across time. Such a position further requires addressing how an apparent unified agency emerges from mental plurality in interaction with the environment across time.

One potentially helpful perspective for addressing this is found within dynamical systems theoretical approaches. According to Richardson, Dale, and Marsh (2014), dynamical systems theory proposes that "the behaviour of a complex dynamical system can arise in a self-organised manner from the free interplay of components and properties of the system" (p. 254). Broadly speaking, dynamical systems are systems whose behaviour evolves or changes over time via continuous interaction throughout all the levels of the developing system (Richardson et al., 2014; Thelen & Smith, 2007). Such systems move beyond predicting simple linear cause-effect relations and address non-linear causal relations and outputs. Here Richardson et al. (2014) write: "A nonlinear system is one in which the system's output is not directly proportional to the input, as opposed to a linear system in which the output can be simply represented as a weighted sum of input components" (p. 256). Highly complex behaviour can emerge then from very simple rules or systems when the components interact with one another in a non-linear manner. This means that "very simple deterministic systems can produce extremely complex and unpredictable behaviour" (Richardson et al., 2014, p. 257).

One implication of this position is that seemingly complex person-level behaviour could arise in a self-organised fashion from the interaction of more primitive components of the personality system (Richardson et al., 2014). An example of such self-organising emergent behavioural patterns is found with ant colonies, whereby organisation emerges but without a central controller: "In each [harvester] ant colony, the queen is merely an egg-layer, not an authority figure, and no ant directs the behaviour of others. Thus the coordinated behaviour of colonies arises from the ways that workers use local information" (Gordon, 2007, p. 279). This is consistent with the view that what appears as complex, sophisticated person-level behaviour can arise from relatively primitive motivational systems rather than from a centralised controller or self-as-agent (cf. Maze, 1983).

The relation between dynamical systems thinking and the use of modelling as proof-of-concept provides one avenue for testing complex theories relevant to understanding trauma-dissociation and DID (Williams, 2018). By way of example, the application of dynamical systems thinking to personality has been particularly useful with respect to the concept of "attractors": "An attractor is a state or subset of states toward which the dynamical system moves over time (i.e., corresponds to a final future state or set of states)" (Richardson et al., 2014, p. 262). In relation to personality development, Nowak, Vallacher, and Zochowski (2005) write:

> The task of the dynamical perspective on personality development is to show how fundamental features of individuality can emerge from interactions among elements comprising psychological systems and features of the environment. Central to this account is the notion of attractor … Attractors capture the interplay between structure and dynamics in a complex system and thus are useful for framing the tension between stability and change in psychological processes.
>
> (p. 352)

The notion of attractor provides a mean of addressing the so-called "personality paradox" (cf. Mischel, 2004), whereby personality is for the most part generally stable over time but can vary according to situation. In this respect, a dynamical systems approach appears well suited for understanding relative stability but also changing patterns of self-organisation with respect to "attractors" and "attractor dynamics":

> The constraints on psychological process can be understood in terms of *attractor dynamics*. An attractor is a state or a reliable pattern of changes (e.g., oscillation between two states) toward which a dynamical system evolves over time, and to which the system returns after it has been perturbed. In a system governed by attractor dynamics, a relatively wide range of starting points (initial states) will eventually converge on a much smaller set of states or on a pattern of change between states. An attractor in effect "attracts" the system's dynamics, so that despite differences at the outset in one's thoughts, feelings, or behaviors, the process unfolds in the direction of the attractor. Attempting to move the system out of its attractor, moreover, promotes forces that reinstate the system at its attractor.
>
> (Nowak et al., 2005, p. 354, their italics)

There are various forms of attractors, including fixed-point attractors acting as a stable, fixed equilibrium point where the system trajectories converge. Fixed point attractors generally have the greatest relevance for personality (Nowak et al., 2005, p. 353) because a single "self" can be seen to act as a common equilibrium point. In this respect, attractor dynamics provide a framework for understanding how personality emerges:

> Framing personality development in terms of attractor dynamics provides the point of departure for theory and research. The most basic question concerns the origins of attractors. It is usually assumed in psychological models ... that attractors are created by the repeated experience of a particular state so that, metaphorically, the state becomes "engraved" in the person's relevant psychological system. In a process somewhat reminiscent of learning, frequent repetition of a particular state paves the way for the system to develop a tendency to converge on this state in the future and to stabilize when in the state.
>
> (Nowak et al., 2005, p. 358)

Nevertheless, several fixed-point attractors can emerge, with some displaying greater dominance than others. As Richardson et al. (2014) write: "A system may have two or more stable fixed points, in which case the system is considered to be *multistable*" (p. 262, their italics). The notion of multiple attractors thus provides a basis for understanding how relatively independent and discrepant dissociative parts could emerge and be maintained. As Nowak et al. (2005) write,

> a person may have multiple fixed-point attractors, each reflecting a characteristic mode of thought, affect, and behavior. These attractors may vary in strength,

so that certain attractors are more likely than others to capture and maintain the dynamics of a person's functioning.

(p. 354)

Various dissociative parts could thus each reflect a fixed point of equilibrium, displaying all the features of personality as seen in DID.

It becomes immediately obvious then that if the self is the emergent pattern and typically dominant pattern, then similar possibilities exist with respect to multiple self-patterns emerging: "The potential for multiple fixed-point attractors captures the idea that people may have different and even conflicting goals, self-views, and behavior patterns" (Nowak, Vallacher & Zochowski, 2005, p. 355). Thus, a dynamical systems approach to personality can potentially address the relative stability of personality, but nevertheless account for changes in personality organisation in terms of dynamic and self-organising systems reflecting DID. If this can be successfully modelled, then we have a preliminary evidence that the theoretical position proposed here is viable.

Conclusion

Understanding how the young mind accommodates traumatic stress is both essential and shrouded in controversy. One major stumbling block in this regard appears to be conceptual in nature. This book has analysed the conceptual and theoretical claims surrounding trauma-dissociation and the possibility for dissociative personality parts. Despite the problems found within the literature, trauma-dissociation is comprehensible as a complex process that interferes with ordinary personality development, and whereby multiple dissociative parts emerge. These dissociative parts are more or less "personalities" to the same extent as the common "self" or ego. In fact, the common view that we consist of a relatively unified self or ego appears, to be a false belief, partly resulting from the limitations of our perceptual apparatus. Instead, the foundations of the mind appear, if anything, to be relatively primitive motivational-affective systems that nevertheless give rise to both the highs and lows found in human activity. Although this thesis would be difficult to convincingly demonstrate, modelling based on dynamical systems approaches can potentially address the complexity involved in the process of traumatisation and the development of personality.

References

Allport, G. W. (1961). *Pattern and growth in personality*. New York: Holt, Rinehart & Wilson.

American Psychiatric Association. (1980). *Diagnostic and statistical manual of mental disorders* (3rd ed.). Washington, DC: APA.

American Psychiatric Association. (1987). *Diagnostic and statistical manual of mental disorders* (3rd ed., rev.). Washington, DC: APA.

American Psychiatric Association. (1994). *Diagnostic and statistical manual of mental disorders* (4th ed.). Washington, DC: APA.

American Psychiatric Association. (2000). *Diagnostic and statistical manual of mental disorders* (4th ed., text rev.). Washington, DC: APA.

American Psychiatric Association. (2013). *Diagnostic and statistical manual of mental disorders* (5th ed.). Washington, DC: APA. https://doi.org/10.1176/appi.books.9780890425596.

American Psychiatric Association. (2022). *Diagnostic and statistical manual of mental disorders* (5th ed., text rev.). Washington, DC: APA. https://doi.org/10.1176/appi.books. 9780890425787.

Amstadter, A. B., & Vernon, L. L. (2008). Emotional reactions during and after trauma: A comparison of trauma types. *Journal of Aggression, Maltreatment & Trauma, 16*, 391–408.

Andersen, S. L., Tomada, A., Vincow, E. S., Valente, E., Polcari, A., & Teicher, M. H. (2008). Preliminary evidence for sensitive periods in the effect of childhood sexual abuse on regional brain development. *The Journal of Neuropsychiatry & Clinical Neurosciences, 20*, 292–301.

Anderson, J. (1962). *Studies in empirical philosophy*. Sydney: Angus & Robertson.

Armstrong, D. M. (1973). *Belief, truth and knowledge*. Cambridge: Cambridge University Press.

Audi, R. (Ed.) (1995). *The Cambridge dictionary of philosophy*. Cambridge: Cambridge University Press.

Baes, N., Vylomova, E., Zyphur, M., & Haslam, N. (2023). The semantic inflation of "trauma" in psychology. *Psychology of Language & Communication, 27*, 23–45.

Bailey, T. D., & Brand, B. L. (2017). Traumatic dissociation: Theory, research, and treatment. *Clinical Psychology: Science and Practice, 24*, 170–185.

Baker, A. J. (1986). *Australian realism*. Cambridge: Cambridge University Press.

Bandura, A. (2002). Social cognitive theory in cultural context. *Applied Psychology: An International Review, 51*, 269–290.

Banicki, K. (2012). Connective conceptual analysis and psychology. *Theory & Psychology, 22*, 310–323.

Baumeister, R. F., Maranges, H. M., & Vohs, K. D. (2018). Human self as information agent: Functioning in a social environment based on shared meanings. *Review of General Psychology, 22*, 36–47.

Bell, P., Staines, P., & Michell, J. (2000). *Logical psych.* Sydney: UNSW Press.

Bennett, M. R., & Hacker, P. M. S. (2003). *Philosophical foundations of neuroscience.* Malden, MA: Blackwell Publishing.

Beres, D. (1962). The unconscious fantasy. *Psychoanalytic Quarterly, 31*, 309–328.

Berridge, K. C. (2004). Motivation concepts in behavioral neuroscience. *Physiology & Behavior, 81*, 179–209.

Berridge, K. C. (2019). Affective valence in the brain: Modules or modes? *Nature Reviews Neuroscience, 20*, 225–234.

Bertocci, P. A. (1945). The psychological self, the ego, and personality. *Psychological Review, 52*, 91–99.

Bhavsar, V., Ventriglio, A., & Bhugra, D. (2016). Dissociative trance and spirit possession: Challenges for cultures in transition. *Psychiatry & Clinical Neurosciences, 70*, 551–559.

Blihar, D., Delgado, E., Buryak, M., Gonzalez, M., & Waechter, R. (2020). A systematic review of the neuroanatomy of dissociative identity disorder. *European Journal of Trauma & Dissociation, 4*, 100148.

Blizard, R. A. (2003). Disorganized attachment, development of dissociated self states, and a relational approach to treatment. *Journal of Trauma & Dissociation, 4*, 27–50.

Boag, S. (2005). Addressing mental plurality: Justification, objections and logical requirements of strongly partitive accounts of mind. *Theory and Psychology, 15*, 747–767.

Boag, S. (2010). Repression, suppression, and conscious awareness. *Psychoanalytic Psychology, 27*, 164–181.

Boag, S. (2011). Explanation in personality research: 'verbal magic' and the five-factor model. *Philosophical Psychology, 24*, 223–243.

Boag, S. (2012). *Freudian repression, the unconscious, and the dynamics of inhibition.* London: Karnac.

Boag, S. (2014). Ego, drives, and the dynamics of internal objects. *Frontiers in Psychoanalysis and Neuropsychoanalysis, 5*, 1–13.

Boag, S. (2015). Personality assessment, 'construct validity', and the significance of theory. *Personality & Individual Differences, 84*, 36–44.

Boag, S. (2015b). In defence of unconscious mentality. In S. Boag, L. A. W. Brakel, & V. Talvitie (Eds.), *Psychoanalysis and philosophy of mind* (pp. 239–265). London: Karnac.

Boag, S. (2017). *Metapsychology and the foundations of psychoanalysis: Attachment, neuropsychoanalysis, and integration.* London: Routledge.

Boag, S. (2018). Personality dynamics, motivation, and the logic of explanation. *Review of General Psychology, 22*, 427–436.

Boag, S. (2020). Reflective awareness, repression, and the cognitive unconscious. *Psychoanalytic Psychology, 37*, 18–27.

Bombay, A., Matheson, K., & Anisman, H. (2009). Intergenerational trauma: Convergence of multiple processes among first nations peoples in Canada. *International Journal of Indigenous Health, 5*, 6–47.

Borsboom, D., Mellenbergh, G. J., & Van Heerden, J. (2003). The theoretical status of latent variables. *Psychological Review, 110*, 203–219.

Bowman, E. S. (2011). Nijenhuis and Van der Hart: One view of the elephant. *Journal of Trauma & Dissociation, 12,* 446–449.

Bowlby, J. (1969). *Attachment and loss: Vol. 1: Attachment.* London: Hogarth.

Bowlby, J. (1973). *Attachment and loss: Vol. 2: Separation.* London: Hogarth.

Bowlby, J. (1980). *Attachment and loss: Vol. 3: Loss.* London: Hogarth.

Bowlby, J. (1982). Attachment and loss: Retrospect and prospect. *American Journal of Orthopsychiatry, 52,* 664–678.

Boysen, G. A. (2011). The scientific status of childhood dissociative identity disorder: A review of published research. *Psychotherapy & Psychosomatics, 80,* 329–334.

Boysen, G. A., & Van Bergen, A. (2013). A review of published research on adult dissociative identity disorder: 2000–2010. *The Journal of Nervous & Mental Disease, 201,* 5–11.

Boysen, G. A., & Van Ross, C. A. (2011). Possession experiences in dissociative identity disorder: A preliminary study. *Journal of Trauma & Dissociation, 12,* 393–400.

Branco, T., & Redgrave, P. (2020). The neural basis of escape behavior in vertebrates. *Annual Review of Neuroscience, 43,* 417–439.

Brakel, L. A. W. (2010). *Unconscious knowing and other essays in psycho-philosophical analysis.* Oxford: Oxford University Press.

Brakel, L. A. W. (2013). *The ontology of psychology.* New York: Routledge.

Brand, B. L., Sar, V., Stavropoulos, P., Krüger, C., Korzekwa, M., Martínez-Taboas, A., & Middleton, W. (2016). Separating fact from fiction: An empirical examination of six myths about dissociative identity disorder. *Harvard Review of Psychiatry, 24*(4), 257–270.

Braude, S. (1991). Multiple personality and the structure of the self. In D. Kolak & R. Martin (Eds.), *Self and identity: Contemporary philosophical issues* (pp. 134–144). New York & Toronto: Macmillan.

Braude, S. E. (2014). The conceptual unity of dissociation: A philosophical argument. In P. F. Dell & J. A. O'Neil (Eds.), *In dissociation and the dissociative disorders: DSM-V and beyond* (pp. 27–36). New York: Routledge.

Brenner, C. (1980). Metapsychology and psychoanalytic theory. *Psychoanalytic Quarterly, 49,* 189–214.

Brentano, F. (1874/1973). *Psychology from an empirical standpoint* (Translated by A. C. Rancurello, D. B. Terrell, & L. L. McAlister). London: Routledge & Kegan Paul.

Breuer, J., & Freud, S. (1895d). *Studies in hysteria (1893–1895). S. E., II.* London: Hogarth.

Bromberg, P. M. (2003). Something wicked this way comes: Trauma, dissociation, and conflict: The space where psychoanalysis, cognitive science, and neuroscience overlap. *Psychoanalytic Psychology, 20,* 558–574.

Brown, R. J. (2006). Different types of "dissociation" have different psychological mechanisms. *Journal of Trauma & Dissociation, 7,* 7–28.

Brown, R. J. (2011). Commentary on "dissociation in trauma: A new definition and comparison with previous formulations" by Nijenhuis and Van der Hart. *Journal of Trauma & Dissociation, 12,* 450–453.

Bucci, W. S. (2016). Divide and multiply: A multi-dimensional view of dissociative processes. In E. Howell & S. Itzkowitz (Eds.), *The dissociative mind in psychoanalysis* (pp. 187–199). London: Routledge.

Buchanan, G., Gewirtz, A. H., Lucke, C., & Wambach, M. R. (2020). The concept of childhood trauma in psychopathology: Definitions and historical perspectives. In G. Spalletta, D. Janiri, F. Piras, & G. Sani (Eds.), *Childhood trauma in mental disorders* (pp. 9–26). Switzerland: Springer, Cham.

Bühler, K. E., & Heim, G. (2009). Psychopathological approaches in Pierre Janet's conception of the subconscious. *Psychopathology, 42,* 190–200.

Cardeña, E. (1994). The domain of dissociation. In S. J. Lynn & J. W. Rhue (Eds.), *Dissociation: Clinical and theoretical perspectives* (pp. 15–31). New York: The Guilford Press.

Cardeña, E. (2011). One split too many.... *Journal of Trauma & Dissociation, 12,* 457–460.

Cardeña, E., & Bowman, E. S. (2011). Defining (structural) dissociation: A debate. *Journal of Trauma & Dissociation, 12,* 413–415.

Cardeña, E., & Carlson, E. (2011). Acute stress disorder revisited. *Annual Review of Clinical Psychology, 7,* 245–267.

Cardeña, E., & Gleaves, D. H. (2007). Dissociative disorders. In M. Hersen, S. M. Turner, & D. C. Beidel (Eds.), *Adult psychopathology and diagnosis* (pp. 473–503). Hoboken, NJ: John Wiley & Sons.

Carver, C. S. (2006). Approach, avoidance, and the self-regulation of affect and action. *Motivation and Emotion, 30,* 105–110.

Cassullo, G. (2019). Janet and Freud: Long-time rivals. In G. Craparo, F. Ortu, & O. Van der Hart (Eds.), *Rediscovering Pierre Janet: Trauma, dissociation, and a new context for psychoanalysis* (pp. 43–52). London: Routledge.

Cavell, M. (1993). *The psychoanalytic mind: From Freud to philosophy.* Cambridge, MA: Harvard University Press.

Cervone, D. (2004). The architecture of personality. *Psychological Review, 111,* 183–204.

Cervone, D. (2005). Personality architecture: Within-person structures and processes. *Annual Review of Psychology, 56,* 423–452.

Chalavi, S., Vissia, E. M., Giesen, M. E., Nijenhuis, E. R., Draijer, N., Cole, J. H., ... & Reinders, A. A. (2015). Abnormal hippocampal morphology in dissociative identity disorder and post-traumatic stress disorder correlates with childhood trauma and dissociative symptoms. *Human Brain Mapping, 36,* 1692–1704.

Cheshire, N., & Thomä, H. (1991). Metaphor, neologism and 'open texture': Implications for translating Freud's scientific thought. *International Review of Psycho-analysis, 18,* 429–454.

Choi, E. A., Husić, M., Millan, E. Z., Gilchrist, S., Power, J. M., dit Bressel, P. J. R., & McNally, G. P. (2022). A corticothalamic circuit trades off speed for safety during decision-making under motivational conflict. *Journal of Neuroscience, 42,* 3473–3483.

Clarke, D. M. (1989). *Occult powers and hypotheses: Cartesian natural philosophy under Louis XIV.* Oxford: Oxford University Press.

Coltheart, M. (2012). The cognitive level of explanation. *Australian Journal of Psychology, 64,* 11–18.

Conway, M. A. (2005). Memory and the self. *Journal of Memory & Language, 53,* 594–628.

Cramer, P. (2000). Defense mechanisms in psychology today: Further processes for adaption. *American Psychologist, 55,* 637–646.

Craparo, G., Ortu, F., & Van der Hart, O. (Eds.) (2019). *Rediscovering Pierre Janet: Trauma, dissociation, and a new context for psychoanalysis.* London: Routledge.

Crews, F. (1995). *The memory wars: Freud's legacy in dispute.* New York: New York Review.

Dalenberg, C. J., Brand, B. L., Gleaves, D. H., Dorahy, M. J., Loewenstein, R. J., Cardena, E., ... & Spiegel, D. (2012). Evaluation of the evidence for the trauma and fantasy models of dissociation. *Psychological Bulletin, 138,* 550–588.

Dalenberg, C. J., Brand, B. L., Loewenstein, R. J., Gleaves, D. H., Dorahy, M. J., Cardeña, E., ... & Spiegel, D. (2014). Reality versus fantasy: Reply to Lynn et al. (2014). *Psychological Bulletin, 140,* 911–920.

Dalenberg, C. J., Straus, E., & Carlson, E. B. (2017). Defining trauma. In S. E. Gold (Ed.), *APA handbook of trauma psychology: Foundations in knowledge* (Vol. 1, pp. 15–33). Washington, DC: American Psychological Association.

Dalenberg, C. J., Brand, B. L., Loewenstein, R. J., Frewen, P. A., & Spiegel, D. (2020). Inviting scientific discourse on traumatic dissociation: Progress made and obstacles to further resolution. *Psychological Injury and Law, 13*, 135–154.

Dalgleish, T., & Power, M. J. (2004). The I of the storm—Relations between self and conscious emotion experience: Comment on Lambie and Marcel (2002). *Psychological Review, 111*, 812–818.

Danieli, Y. (2009). Massive trauma and the healing role of reparative justice. *Journal of Traumatic Stress, 22*, 351–357.

Dell, P. F. (2009). The phenomena of pathological dissociation. In P. F. Dell & J. A. O'Neil (Eds.), *Dissociation and the dissociative disorders: DSM-V and beyond* (pp. 225–237). London: Routledge.

Dell, P. F. (2011). An excellent definition of structural dissociation and a dogmatic rejection of all other models. *Journal of Trauma and Dissociation, 12*, 461–464.

Dell, P. F. (2013). Three dimensions of dissociative amnesia. *Journal of Trauma & Dissociation, 14*, 25–39.

Dennett, D. (1988). Conditions of personhood. In M. F. Goodman (Ed.), *What is a person?* (pp. 145–167). Totowa, NJ: Humana Press.

Denton, R., Frogley, C., Jackson, S., John, M., & Querstret, D. (2017). The assessment of developmental trauma in children and adolescents: A systematic review. *Clinical Child Psychology and Psychiatry, 22*, 260–287.

Diamond, S., Balvin, R. S., & Diamond, F. R. (1963). *Inhibition and choice: A neurobehavioral approach to the problems of plasticity in behaviour*. New York: Harper & Row.

Diseth, T. H. (2005). Dissociation in children and adolescents as reaction to trauma. *Nordic Journal of Psychology, 59*, 79–91.

Dorahy, M. J., Brand, B. L., Şar, V., Krüger, C., Stavropoulos, P., Martínez-Taboas, A., Lewis-Fernández, R., & Middleton, W. (2014). Dissociative identity disorder: An empirical overview. *Australian & New Zealand Journal of Psychiatry, 48*, 402–417.

Dorahy, M. J., & Van der Hart, O. (2007). Relationship between trauma and dissociation: A historical analysis. In E. Vermetten, M. Dorahy, & D. Spiegel (Eds.), *Traumatic dissociation: Neurobiology and treatment* (pp. 3–30). American Psychiatric Publishing, Inc.

Drever, J. (1952). *A dictionary of psychology*. Middlesex: Penguin Books Ltd.

Dweck, C. S. (2017). From needs to goals and representations: Foundations for a unified theory of motivation, personality, and development. *Psychological Review, 124*(6), 689–719.

Eagle, M. (2000a). Repression: Part II. *Psychoanalytic Review, 87*, 161–187.

Edmondson, D., Chaudoir, S. R., Mills, M. A., Park, C. L., Holub, J., & Bartkowiak, J. M. (2011). From shattered assumptions to weakened worldviews: Trauma symptoms signal anxiety buffer disruption. *Journal of Loss and Trauma, 16*, 358–385.

Ellenberger, H. F. (1970). *The discovery of the unconscious: The history and evolution of dynamic psychiatry*. New York: Basic Books.

Elliot, A. J. (2008). Approach and avoidance motivation. In A. J. Elliot (Ed.), *Handbook of approach and avoidance motivation* (pp. 3–14). New York: Psychology Press.

Erdelyi, M. H. (1985). *Psychoanalysis: Freud's cognitive psychology*. New York: W. H. Freeman & Co.

Erdelyi, M. H. (1986). Experimental indeterminancies in the dissociation paradigm of subliminal perception. *Behavioral & Brain Sciences, 9*, 30–31.

Erdelyi, M. H. (1990). Repression, reconstruction, and defence: History and integration of the psychoanalytic and experimental frameworks. In J. L. Singer (Ed.), *Repression and dissociation: Implications for personality theory, psychopathology, and health* (pp. 1–31). Chicago: University of Chicago Press.

Erdelyi, M. H. (2004). Subliminal perception and its cognates: Theory, indeterminancy, and time. *Consciousness & Cognition, 13*, 73–91.

Fairbairn, W. R. D. (1952). *Psychoanalytic studies of the personality*. London: Tavistock.

Frampton, M. F. (1991). Considerations on the role of Brentano's concept of intentionality in Freud's repudiation of the seduction theory. *International Review of Psycho-analysis, 18*, 27–36.

Frewen, P., Brand, B., & Lanius, R. (2022). Reply to Dr. Nijenhuis: Differentiating dissociation from distress. *Journal of Trauma & Dissociation, 23*, 581–583.

Follette, V. M., & Vijay, A. (2009). Mindfulness for trauma and posttraumatic stress disorder. In F. Didonna (Ed.), *Clinical handbook of mindfulness* (pp. 299–317). New York: Springer.

Forrest, K. A. (2001). Toward an etiology of dissociative identity disorder: A neurodevelopmental approach. *Consciousness & Cognition, 10*, 259–293.

Freud, A. (1968). *The ego and the mechanisms of defence*. London: The Hogarth Press.

Freud, S. (1888). Hysteria. *S. E., 1*: 39–59. London: Hogarth.

Freud, S. (1894a). The neuro-psychoses of defence. *S. E., 3*: 41–61. London: Hogarth.

Freud, S. (1895f). A reply to criticisms of my paper on anxiety neurosis. *S. E., 3*: 119–139. London: Hogarth.

Freud, S. (1896a). Heredity and the aetiology of the neuroses. *S. E., 3*: 143–156. London: Hogarth.

Freud, S. (1899). Screen memories. *S. E., 3*: 299–232. London: Hogarth.

Freud, S. (1900a). The interpretation of dreams. *S. E., 4–5*. London: Hogarth.

Freud, S. (1901b). The psychopathology of everyday life. *S. E., 6*. London: Hogarth.

Freud, S. (1905c). Jokes and their relation to the unconscious. *S. E., 8*. London: Hogarth.

Freud, S. (1905e). Fragment of an analysis of a case of hysteria. *S. E., 7*: 1–122. London: Hogarth.

Freud, S. (1906a). My views on the part played by sexuality in the aetiology of the neuroses. *S. E., 7*: 269–279. London: Hogarth.

Freud, S (1907a). Delusions and dreams in Jensen's *Gradiva*. *S. E., 9*: 1–96. London: Hogarth.

Freud, S. (1909d). Notes upon a case of obsessional neurosis. *S. E., 10*: 151–138. London: Hogarth.

Freud, S. (1910a). Five lectures on psycho-analysis. *S. E., 11*: 1–56. London: Hogarth.

Freud, S. (1910i). The psycho-analytic view of the psychogenic disturbance of vision. *S. E., 11*: 209–218. London: Hogarth.

Freud, S. (1910k). 'Wild' psycho-analysis. *S. E., 11*: 219–228. London: Hogarth.

Freud, S. (1911b). Formulations on the two principles of mental functioning. *S. E., 12*: 213–226. London: Hogarth.

Freud, S. (1911c). Psycho-analytic notes on an autobiographical account of a case of paranoia (Dementia paranoides). *S. E., 12*: 3–82. London: Hogarth.

Freud, S (1912b). The dynamics of transference. *S. E., 12*: 97–108. London: Hogarth.

Freud, S. (1912f). Contributions to a discussion on masturbation. *S. E.*, *12*: 239–254. London: Hogarth.

Freud, S. (1912g). A note on the unconscious in psycho-analysis. *S. E.*, *12*: 256–266. London: Hogarth.

Freud, S. (1912–1913). Totem and taboo. *S. E.*, *13*. London: Hogarth.

Freud, S. (1913j). The claims of psycho-analysis to scientific interest. *S. E.*, *13*: 163–190. London: Hogarth.

Freud, S. (1913m). On psycho-analysis. *S. E.*, *12*: 205–212. London: Hogarth.

Freud, S. (1914a). Fausse reconnaissance ('Déjà Raconté') in psycho-analytic treatment. *S. E.*, *13*: 199–207. London: Hogarth.

Freud, S. (1914c). On narcissism: An introduction. *S. E.*, *14*: 67–102. London: Hogarth.

Freud, S. (1914d). On the history of the psycho-analytic movement. *S. E.*, *14*: 1–66. London: Hogarth.

Freud, S. (1915a). Observations on transference-love (further recommendations on the technique of psycho-analysis III). *S. E.*, *12*: 157–174. London: Hogarth.

Freud, S. (1915c). Instincts and their vicissitudes. *S. E.*, *14*: 109–140. London: Hogarth.

Freud, S. (1915d). Repression. *S. E.*, *14*: 141–158. London: Hogarth.

Freud, S. (1915e). The unconscious. *S. E.*, *14*: 159–215. London: Hogarth.

Freud, S. (1916–1917). Introductory lectures on psycho-analysis. *S. E.*, *15–16*. London: Hogarth.

Freud, S. (1917d). A metapsychological supplement to the theory of dreams. *S. E.*, *15*. London: Hogarth.

Freud, S. (1919g). Preface to Reik's *ritual: Psycho-analytic studies*. *S. E.*, *17*: 257–264. London: Hogarth.

Freud, S. (1920g). Beyond the pleasure *principle*. *S. E.*, *18*: 1–64. London: Hogarth.

Freud, S. (1923a). Two encyclopaedia articles. *S. E.*, *18*: 233–260. London: Hogarth.

Freud, S. (1923b). The ego and the Id. *S. E.*, *19*: 1–66. London: Hogarth.

Freud, S. (1924c). The economic problem of masochism. *S. E.*, *19*: 155–170. London: Hogarth.

Freud, S. (1924f). A short account of psycho-analysis. *S. E.*, *19*: 189–210. London: Hogarth.

Freud, S. (1925d). An autobiographical study. *S. E.*, *20*: 1–74. London: Hogarth.

Freud, S. (1925e). The resistances to psycho-analysis. *S. E.*, *19*: 211–224. London: Hogarth.

Freud, S. (1925i). Some additional notes on dream-interpretation as a whole. *S. E.*, *19*: 124–138. London: Hogarth.

Freud, S. (1926d). Inhibitions, symptoms and anxiety. *S. E.*, *20*: 75–176. London: Hogarth.

Freud, S. (1926e). The question of lay analysis. *S. E.*, *29*: 177–258. London: Hogarth.

Freud, S. (1926f). Psycho-analysis. *S. E.*, *20*: 259–270. London: Hogarth.

Freud, S. (1927a). Postscript to *The question of lay analysis*. *S. E.*, *20*: 251–258. London: Hogarth.

Freud, S. (1933a). New introductory lectures on psycho-analysis. *S. E.*, *22*. London: Hogarth.

Freud, S. (1936a). A disturbance of memory on the acropolis. *S. E.*, *22*: 237–248. London: Hogarth.

Freud, S. (1937c). Analysis terminable and interminable. *S. E.*, *23*: 209–254. London: Hogarth.

Freud, S. (1937d). Constructions in analysis. *S. E.*, *23*: 255–270. London: Hogarth.

Freud, S. (1939a). Moses and monotheism: Three essays. *S. E.*, *23*: 1–138. London: Hogarth.

Freud, S. (1940a). An outline of psycho-analysis. *S. E.*, *23*: 1–138. London: Hogarth.

Freud, S. (1950). A project for a scientific psychology. *S. E., 1*: 283–397. London: Hogarth.

Freud, S. (1950a). Extracts from the Fliess papers. *S. E., 1*: 175–280. London: Hogarth.

Freud, A. (1968). *The ego and the mechanisms of defence*. London: The Hogarth Press.

Gardner, S. (1993). *Irrationality and the philosophy of psychoanalysis*. Cambridge: Cambridge University Press.

Gay, V. P. (1982). Semiotics as metapsychology: The status of repression. *Bulletin of the Menninger Clinic, 46*, 489–506.

Gobin, R. L., & Freyd, J. J. (2014). The impact of betrayal trauma on the tendency to trust. *Psychological trauma: Theory, research, practice, & policy, 6*, 505–511.

Gordon, D. M. (2007). Control without hierarchy. *Nature, 446*, 143–143.

Grossman, W. I. (1982). The self as fantasy: Fantasy as theory. *Journal of the American Psychoanalytic Association, 30*, 919–937.

Gullestad, S. E. (2005). Who is 'who' in dissociation? A plea for psychodynamics in a time of trauma. *The International Journal of Psychoanalysis, 86*, 639–656.

Hamburger, A. (2021). The complexity of social trauma diagnosis and intervention. In A. Hamburger, C. Hancheva, & V. D. Volken (Eds.), *Social trauma–An interdisciplinary textbook* (pp. 55–67). Cham, Switzerland: Springer.

Hart, B. (1910). The conception of the subconscious. *The Journal of Abnormal Psychology, 4*, 351–371.

Hartmann, H. (1950). Comments on the psychoanalytic theory of the ego. *The Psychoanalytic Study of the Child, 5*, 74–96.

Haslam, N. (2016). Concept creep: Psychology's expanding concepts of harm and pathology. *Psychological Inquiry, 27*, 1–17.

Heil, J. (1989). Minds divided. *Mind, 98*, 571–583.

Heim, G., & Bühler, K. E. (2006). Psychological trauma and fixed ideas in Pierre Janet's conception of dissociative disorders. *American Journal of Psychotherapy, 60*, 111–129.

Heim, G., & Bühler, K. E. (2019). Pierre Janet's views on the etiology, pathogenesis, and therapy of dissociative disorders. In G. Craparo, F. Ortu, & O. Van der Hart (Eds.), *Rediscovering Pierre Janet: Trauma, dissociation, and a new context for psychoanalysis* (pp. 178–199). London: Routledge.

Henderson, L. (1972). On mental energy. *British Journal of Psychology, 63*, 1–7.

Hendrickson, K. M., McCarty, T., & Goodwin, J. (1990). Animal alters. *Dissociation, 3*, 218–221.

Henriques, G. (2019). Toward a metaphysical empirical psychology. In T. Teo (Ed.), *Re-envisioning theoretical psychology: Diverging ideas and practices* (pp. 209–237). Cham, Switzerland: Springer International Publishing.

Hibberd, F. J. (2014). The metaphysical basis of a process psychology. *Journal of Theoretical and Philosophical Psychology, 34*, 161–186.

Hilgard, E. R. (1977). *Divided consciousness: Multiple controls in human thought and action*. New York: Wiley.

Hodges, M., Godbout, N., Briere, J., Lanktree, C., Gilbert, A., & Kletzka, N. T. (2013). Cumulative trauma and symptom complexity in children: A path analysis. *Child Abuse & Neglect, 37*, 891–898.

Hoeldtke, R. (1967). The history of associationism and British medical psychology. *Medical History, 11*, 46–65.

Holmes, E. A., et al. (2005). Are there two qualitatively distinct forms of dissociation? A review & some clinical implications. *Clinical Psychology Review, 25*, 1–23.

Holmes, J. (2003). Borderline personality disorder and the search for meaning: An attachment perspective. *Australian & New Zealand Journal of Psychiatry, 37*, 524–531.

Hopkins, J. (1988). Epistemology and depth psychology: Critical notes on *The Foundations of Psycho-analysis*. In P. Clark & C. Wright (Eds.), *Mind, psychoanalysis and science* (pp. 33–60). Oxford: Basil Blackwell.

Howell, E. (2005). *The dissociative mind*. Hillsdale, NJ: Analytic Press.

Howell, E., & Itzkowitz, S. (2016a). Is trauma-analysis psychoanalysis? In E. Howell, & S. Itzkowitz (Eds.), *The dissociative mind in psychoanalysis: Understanding and working with trauma* (pp. 7–19). London: Routledge.

Howell, E., & Itzkowitz, S. (2016b). From trauma-analysis to psychoanalysis and back again. In E. Howell & S. Itzkowitz (Eds.), *The dissociative mind in psychoanalysis: Understanding and working with trauma* (pp. 20–32). London: Routledge.

Howell, E., & Itzkowitz, S. (2016c). The everywhereness of trauma and the dissociative structuring of the mind. In E. Howell, & S. Itzkowitz (Eds.), *The dissociative mind in psychoanalysis: Understanding and working with trauma* (pp. 33–43). London: Routledge.

Hughes, K., Bellis, M. A., Hardcastle, K. A., Sethi, D., Butchart, A., Mikton, C., Jones, L., & Dunne, M. P. (2017). The effect of multiple adverse childhood experiences on health: A systematic review and meta-analysis. *The Lancet Public Health, 2*, e356–e366.

Hume, D. (1911/1739). *A treatise of human nature* (Vol. 1). London: J. M. Dent & Sons

Igreja, V., Dias-Lambranca, B., Hershey, D. A., Racin, L., Richters, A., & Reis, R. (2010). The epidemiology of spirit possession in the aftermath of mass political violence in Mozambique. *Social Science & Medicine, 71*, 592–599.

Immergluck, L. (1964). Determinism-freedom in contemporary psychology: An ancient problem revisited. *American Psychologist, 19*, 270–281.

International Society for the Study of Trauma and Dissociation. (2011). Guidelines for treating dissociative identity disorder in adults, third revision. *Journal of Trauma & Dissociation, 12*, 115–187.

James, W. (1884/1965). The dilemma of determinism. In P. Edwards & A. Pap. (Eds.), *A modern introduction to philosophy* (pp. 25–37). New York: Free Press.

James, W. (1890/1950). *The principles of psychology* (Vol. I). New York: H. Holt and Company.

Janet, P. (1901). *The mental state of hystericals: A study of mental stigmata and mental accidents*. New York: G. P. Putnam's Sons.

Janet, P. (1907a). *The major symptoms of hysteria*. New York: Macmillan Publishers.

Janet, P. (1907b). A symposium on the subconscious. *The Journal of Abnormal Psychology, 2*, 58–67.

Jones, E., & Wessely, S. (2006). Psychological trauma: A historical perspective. *Psychiatry, 5*, 217–220.

Jureidini, J. (2004). Does dissociation offer a useful explanation for psychopathology? *Psychopathology, 37*, 259–265.

Kane, R. (Ed.). (2002). *The Oxford handbook of free will*. Oxford: Oxford University Press.

Kelly, G. A. (1955). *The psychology of personal constructs* (2 volumes). New York: Norton.

Kernberg, O. F. (2022). Some implications of new developments in neurobiology for psychoanalytic object relations theory. *Neuropsychoanalysis, 24*, 3–12.

Kihlstrom, J. F. (1987). The cognitive unconscious. *Science, 237*, 1445–1452.

Kihlstrom, J. F. (2005). Dissociative disorders. *Annual Review of Clinical Psychology, 1*, 227–253.

Kinniburgh, K. J., Blaustein, M., Spinazzola, J., & Van der Kolk, B. A. (2005). Attachment, self-regulation, and competency. *Psychiatric Annals, 35*, 424–430.

Kirmayer, L. J., Adeponle, A., & Dzokoto, V. A. A. (2018). Varieties of global psychology: Cultural diversity and constructions of the self. In s. Fernando & R. Moodley (Eds.), *Global psychologies: Mental health and the Global South* (pp. 21–37).

Kirsch, M. (2019). On the abilities of unconscious Freudian motivational drives to evoke conscious emotions. *Frontiers in Psychology, 10*, 441323.

Klein, S. B. (2010). The self: As a construct in psychology and neuropsychological evidence for its multiplicity. *Cognitive Science, 1*, 172–183.

Kluft, R. P. (1996). Treating the traumatic memories of patients with dissociative identity disorder. *The American Journal of Psychiatry, 153*, 103–110.

Kluft, R. P. (2000). The psychoanalytic psychotherapy of dissociative identity disorder in the context of trauma therapy. *Psychoanalytic Inquiry, 20*, 259–286.

Kluft, R. P. (2006). Dealing with alters: A pragmatic clinical perspective. *Psychiatric Clinics, 29*, 281–304.

Knezevic, E., Nenic, K., Milanovic, V., & Knezevic, N. N. (2023). The role of cortisol in chronic stress, neurodegenerative diseases, and psychological disorders. *Cells, 12*(23), 2726.

Kohut, H. (1971). The analysis of the self: a systematic approach to the psychoanalytic treatment of narcissistic personality disorders. New York: International Universities Press.

Lambie, J. A., & Marcel, A. J. (2002). Consciousness and the varieties of emotion experience: A theoretical framework. *Psychological Review, 109*, 219–259.

Lamiell, J. T. (2007). On sustaining critical discourse with mainstream personality investigators problems and prospects. *Theory & Psychology, 17*, 169–185.

Lamiell, J. T. (2013). Statisticism in personality psychologists' use of trait constructs: What is it? How was it contracted? Is there a cure? *New Ideas in Psychology, 31*, 65–71.

Laplanche, J., & Pontalis, J.-B. (1973). *The language of psychoanalysis*. London: Karnac.

LeDoux, J. E. (1990). *The emotional brain*. New York: Simon & Schuster.

LeDoux, J. E. (1995). Emotion: Clues from the brain. *Annual Review of Psychology, 46*, 209–235.

LeDoux, J. E. (2009). The human amygdala: Insights from other animals. In P. J. Whalen & E. A. Phelps (Eds.), *The human amygdala* (pp. 43–60). New York: Guilford Press.

Leising, D., Rogers, K., & Ostner, J. (2009). The undisordered personality: Normative assumptions underlying personality disorder diagnoses. *Review of General Psychology, 13*, 230–241.

Lesley, J., & Varvin, S. (2016). 'Janet vs Freud' on traumatization: A critique of the theory of structural dissociation from an object relations perspective. *British Journal of Psychotherapy, 32*, 436–455.

Lesley, J., & Varvin, S. (2017). 'Janet vs Freud' on traumatization: A critique of the theory of structural dissociation from an object relations perspective. Response. *British Journal of Psychotherapy, 33*, 555–557.

Lilienfeld, S. O., Kirsch, I., Sarbin, T. R., Lynn, S. J., Chaves, J. F., Ganaway, G. K., & Powell, R. A. (1999). Dissociative identity disorder and the sociocognitive model: Recalling the lessons of the past. *Psychological Bulletin, 125*, 507–523.

Liotti, G. (2004). Trauma, dissociation, and disorganized attachment: Three strands of a single braid. *Psychotherapy: Theory, Research, Practice, Training, 41*, 472–486.

Liotti, M., & Panksepp, J. (2004). Imaging human emotions and affective feelings: Implications for biological psychiatry. In J. Panksepp (Ed.), *Textbook of biological psychiatry* (pp. 33–74). Hoboken, NJ: Wiley-Liss.

Lynn, S. J., Lilienfeld, S. O., Merckelbach, H., Giesbrecht, T., McNally, R. J., Loftus, E. F., Bruck, M., Garry, M., & Malaktaris, A. (2014). The trauma model of dissociation: inconvenient truths and stubborn fictions. Comment on Dalenberg et al. (2012). *Psychological Bulletin, 140*, 896–910.

Lynn, S. J., Maxwell, R., Merckelbach, H., Lilienfeld, S. O., van Heugten-van der Kloet, D., & Miskovic, V. (2019). Dissociation and its disorders: Competing models, future directions, and a way forward. *Clinical Psychology Review, 73*, 101755.

Machado, A., & Silva, F. J. (2007). Toward a richer view of the scientific method: The role of conceptual analysis. *American Psychologist, 62*, 671–681.

Mackay, N. (1996). The place of motivation in psychoanalysis. *Modern Psychoanalysis, 21*, 3–17.

Mackay, N. (1997). Constructivism and the logic of explanation. *Journal of Constructivist Psychology, 10*, 339–361.

Mackay, N. (1999). Reason, cause, and rationality in psychological explanation. *Journal of Theoretical and Philosophical Psychology, 19*, 1–21.

Mackay, N. (2002). Desire, symbol, enactment, and some puzzles about the concepts of phantasy and substitute satisfaction. *Modern Psychoanalysis, 27*, 3–11.

Mackay, N., & Petocz, A. (Eds.). (2010). *Realism and psychology: Collected essays*. Leiden: Brill.

Mackie, J. L. (1974). *The cement of the universe: A study of causation*. Oxford: Oxford University Press.

Macmillan, M. (1991). *Freud evaluated: The completed arc*. North-Holland: Elsevier Science Publishers.

Macmurray, J. (1961). *Persons in relation*. New York: Harper & Brothers.

Macmurray, J. (1969). *The self as agent*. London: Faber and Faber.

Madison, P. (1961). *Freud's concept of repression and defense: Its theoretical and observational language*. Minneapolis: University of Minnesota Press.

Main, M., & Solomon, J. (1986). Discovery of an insecure-disorganized/disorientated attachment pattern. In T. B. Brazelton & M. Y. Yogman (Eds.), *Affective development in infancy* (pp. 95–124). Norwood, NJ: Ablex Publishing Corporation.

Malezieux, M., Klein, A. S., & Gogolla, N. (2023). Neural circuits for emotion. *Annual Review of Neuroscience, 46*, 211–231.

Mangiulli, I., Otgaar, H., Jelicic, M., & Merckelbach, H. (2022). A critical review of case studies on dissociative amnesia. *Clinical Psychological Science, 10*, 191–211.

Manning, M. L., & Manning, R. L. (2007). Legion theory: A meta-psychology. *Theory & Psychology, 17*, 839–862.

Markus, H. R., & Kitayama, S. (2010). Cultures and selves: A cycle of mutual constitution. *Perspectives on Psychological Science, 5*, 420–430.

Marques, L., Robinaugh, D. J., LeBlanc, N. J., & Hinton, D. (2011). Cross-cultural variations in the prevalence and presentation of anxiety disorders. *Expert Review of Neurotherapeutics, 11*, 313–322.

Martin, J., Sugarman, J., & Thompson, J. (2003). *Psychology and the question of agency*. Albany: SUNY Press.

Martínez-Taboas, A., Dorahy, M., Sar, V., Middleton, W., & Krüger, C. (2013). Growing not dwindling: International research on the worldwide phenomenon of dissociative disorders. *Journal of Nervous & Mental Disease, 201*, 353–354.

Masson, J. M. (Ed.) (1985). *The complete letters of Sigmund Freud and Wilhelm Fliess, 1887-1904*. Cambridge: Belknap Press.

Mayr, E. (1974). Teleological and teleonomic, a new analysis. In R. S. Cohen & M. W. Wartofsky (Eds.), *Methodological and historical essays in the natural and social sciences* (pp. 91–117). Dordrecht: Springer.

Maze, J. R. (1954). Do intervening variables intervene? *Psychological Review, 61*, 226–234.

Maze, J. R. (1983). *The meaning of behaviour*. London: Allen & Unwin.

Maze, J. R. (1987). The composition of the ego in a deterministic psychology. In W. J. Baker, M. E. Hyland, H. Van Rappard, & A. W. Staats (Eds.), *Current issues in theoretical psychology* (pp. 189–199). North Holland: Elsevier Science Publishers.

Maze, J. R. (1993). The complementarity of object-relations and instinct theory. *International Journal of Psycho-analysis, 74*, 459–70.

Maze, J. R., & Henry, R. M. (1996). Problems in the concept of repression and proposals for their resolution. *International Journal of Psycho-analysis, 77*, 1085–1100.

Maze, J. R. (2001). Social constructionism, deconstructionism and some requirements of discourse. *Theory & Psychology, 11*, 393–417.

McAdams, D. P. (2001). The psychology of life stories. *Review of General Psychology, 5*, 100–122.

McAdams, D. P. (2013). The psychological self as actor, agent, and author. *Perspectives on Psychological Science, 8*, 272–295.

McConnell, A. R. (2011). The multiple self-aspects framework: Self-concept representation and its implications. *Personality and Social Psychology Review, 15*, 3–27.

McCrae, R. R. (2004). Human nature and culture: A trait perspective. *Journal of Research in Personality, 38*, 3–14.

McCrae, R. R., & Costa Jr., P. T. (1995). Trait explanations in personality psychology. *European Journal of Personality, 9*, 231–252.

McCrae, R. R., & Costa Jr., P. T. (2008). Empirical and theoretical status of the five-factor model of personality traits. In G. Boyle, G. Matthews, & D. Daklofske (Eds.), *Sage handbook of personality theory and assessment* (pp. 273–294). Los Angeles, CA: Sage.

McCrae, R. R., & Costa Jr., P. T. (2021). Understanding persons: From stern's personalistics to five-factor theory. *Personality & Individual Differences, 169*, 109816.

McMullen, T. (1982). A critique of humanistic psychology. Australian *Journal of Psychology, 34*, 221–229.

McMullen, T. (1996). Psychology and realism. In C. R. Latimer & J. Michell (Eds.), *At once scientific and philosophic: A Festschrift for John Philip Sutcliffe* (pp. 59–66). Brisbane: Boombana.

McMullen, T. (2018). Memory and its offspring: Realism and the "specious present". *Theory & Psychology, 28*, 172–192.

McNally, G. P. (2021). Motivational competition and the paraventricular thalamus. *Neuroscience & Biobehavioral Reviews, 125*, 193–207.

McNally, R. J. (2003a). Psychological mechanisms in acute response to trauma. *Biological Psychiatry, 53*, 779–788.

McNally, R. J. (2003b). Progress and controversy in the study of posttraumatic stress disorder. *Annual Review of Psychology, 54*, 229–252.

McNally, R. J. (2007). Betrayal trauma theory: A critical appraisal. *Memory, 15*, 280–294.

McNally, R. J. (2007, September). Dispelling confusion about traumatic dissociative amnesia. *Mayo Clinic Proceedings, 82*, 1083–1087.

McNally, R. J. (2010). Can we salvage the concept of psychological trauma? *The Psychologist, 23*, 386–389.

Meissner, W. W. (2003). Mind, brain, and self in psychoanalysis: II. Freud and the mind-body relation. *Psychoanalysis and Contemporary Thought, 26*, 321–344,

Merckelbach, H., Devilly, G. J., & Rassin, E. (2002). Alters in dissociative identity disorder: Metaphors or genuine entities? *Clinical Psychology Review, 22*, 481–497.

Metcalfe, J., & Shimamura, A. P. (1994). *Metacognition: Knowing about knowing.* Cambridge: MIT Press.

Metzinger, T. (2003). *Being no one: The self-model theory of subjectivity*. Cambridge: MIT Press.

Michell, J. (1988). Maze's direct realism and the character of cognition. *Australian Journal of Psychology, 40*, 227–249.

Middleton, W. (2014). Parent-child incest that extends into adulthood: A survey of international press reports, 2007-2012. In V. Şar, W. Middleton, & M. Dorahy (Eds.), *Global perspectives on dissociative disorders: Individual and societal oppression* (pp. 45–64). London: Routledge.

Mischel, W. (2004). Toward an integrative science of the person. *Annual Review of Psychology, 55*, 1–22.

Misslin, R. (2003). The defense system of fear: Behavior and neurocircuitry. *Neurophysiologie Clinique/Clinical Neurophysiology, 33*, 55–66.

Moleiro, C. (2018). Culture and psychopathology: New perspectives on research, practice, and clinical training in a globalized world. *Frontiers in Psychiatry, 9*, 400849.

Moors, A., & de Houwer, J. (2006). Automaticity: A theoretical and conceptual analysis. *Psychological Bulletin, 132*, 297–326.

Nemeroff, C. B. (2016). Paradise lost: The neurobiological and clinical consequences of child abuse and neglect. *Neuron, 89*, 892–909.

Neu, J. (1988). Divided minds: Sartre's "bad faith" critique of Freud. *Review of Metaphysics, 42*, 79–101.

Nijenhuis, E. R. S. (2012). Consciousness and self-consciousness in dissociative disorders. In V. Sinason (Ed.), *Trauma, dissociation, and multiplicity: Working on identity and selves* (pp. 111–154). New York: Routledge.

Nijenhuis, E. R. S. (2015). Boundaries on the concepts of dissociation and dissociative parts of the personality: Required and viable. *Psichiatria e Psicoterapia, 34*, 55–85.

Nijenhuis, E. R. (2019). The metaphor of dissociation: Teleological, phenomenological, structural, dynamical. *Quaderni Di Psicoterapia Cognitiva, 44*, 72–105.

Nijenhuis, E. R. S. (2022). The need to constrain the concept of dissociation. *Journal of Trauma & Dissociation, 23*, 578–580.

Nijenhuis, E. R., & Van der Hart, O. (2011). Dissociation in trauma: A new definition and comparison with previous formulations. *Journal of Trauma and Dissociation, 12*, 416–445.

Nijenhuis, E., Van der Hart, O., & Steele, K. (2010). Trauma-related structural dissociation of the personality. *Activitas Nervosa Superior, 52*, 1–23.

Nijenhuis, E. R. S., Vanderlinden, J., & Spinhoven, P. (1998). Animal defensive reactions as a model for trauma-induced dissociative reactions. *Journal of Traumatic Stress, 11*, 243–260.

Nisbett, R. E., & Wilson, T. D. (1977). Telling more than we know: Verbal reports on mental processes. *Psychological Review, 84*, 231–259.

Nowak, A., Vallacher, R. R., & Zochowski, M. (2005). The emergence of personality: Dynamic foundations of individual variation. *Developmental Review, 25*, 351–385.

Nunes, T., Bryant, P., Barros, R., & Sylva, K. (2012). The relative importance of two different mathematical abilities to mathematical achievement. *British Journal of Educational Psychology, 82*, 136–156.

Öhman, A. (2005). The role of the amygdala in human fear: Automatic detection of threat. *Psychoneuroendocrinology, 30*, 953–958.

Öhman, A. (2009). Human fear conditioning and the amygdala. In P. J. Whalen & E. A. Phelps (Eds.), *The human amygdala* (pp. 118–154). New York: Guilford Press.

Öhman, A., Carlsson, K., Lundqvist, D., & Ingvar, M. (2007). On the unconscious subcortical origin of human fear. *Physiology & Behaviour, 92*, 180–185.

O'Neil, W. M. (1982). *The beginnings of modern psychology*. Sydney: Sydney University Press (Originally published in 1968).

Oppenheimer, L. (2002). Self or selves? Dissociative identity disorder and complexity of the self-system. *Theory & Psychology, 12*, 97–128.

Ortu, F., & Craparo, G. (2019). From consciousness to subconsciousness: A Janetian perspective. In G. Craparo, F. Ortu, & O. Van der Hart (Eds.), *Rediscovering Pierre Janet: Trauma, dissociation, and a new context for psychoanalysis* (pp. 28–40). London: Routledge.

Otgaar, H., Howe, M. L., Patihis, L., Merckelbach, H., Lynn, S. J., Lilienfeld, S. O., & Loftus, E. F. (2019). The return of the repressed: The persistent and problematic claims of long-forgotten trauma. *Perspectives on Psychological Science, 14*, 1072–1095.

Owens, T. J., Robinson, D. T., & Smith-Lovin, L. (2010). Three faces of identity. *Annual Review of Sociology, 36*, 477–499.

Öz, G., Seaquist, E. R., Kumar, A., Criego, A. B., Benedict, L. E., Rao, J. P., ... & Gruetter, R. (2007). Human brain glycogen content and metabolism: Implications on its role in brain energy metabolism. *American Journal of Physiology-Endocrinology & Metabolism, 292*, E946–E951.

Öztürk, E., & Şar, V. (2016). Formation and functions of alter personalities in dissociative identity disorder: A theoretical and clinical elaboration. *Journal of Psychology & Clinical Psychiatry, 6*, 00385.

Öztürk, E., & Sar, V. (2016). Formation and functions of alter personalities in dissociative identity disorder: A theoretical and clinical elaboration. *Journal of Psychology & Clinical Psychiatry, 6*, 1–7.

Panksepp, J. (1999). Emotions as viewed by psychoanalysis and neuroscience: An exercise in consilience. *Neuro-psychoanalysis, 1*, 15–38.

Panksepp, J. (2001). The long-term psychobiological consequences of infant emotions: Prescriptions for the twenty-first century. *Infant Mental Health Journal, 22*, 132–173.

Panksepp, J. (2003). At the interface of the affective, behavioural, and cognitive neurosciences: Decoding the emotional feelings of the brain. *Brain & Cognition, 52*, 4–14.

Panksepp, J. (2005). Affective consciousness: Core emotional feelings in animals and humans. *Consciousness & Cognition, 14*, 30–80.

Panksepp, J., & Biven, L. (2012). *The archaeology of mind: Neuroevolutionary origins of human emotions*. New York: WW Norton & Company.

Panksepp, J., Clarici, A., Vandekerckhove, M., & Yovell, Y. (2019). Neuro-evolutionary foundations of infant minds: From psychoanalytic visions of how primal emotions guide constructions of human minds toward affective neuroscientific understanding of emotions and their disorders. *Psychoanalytic Inquiry, 39*, 36–51.

Panksepp, J., & Moskal, J. (2008). Dopamine and SEEKING: Subcortical "reward" systems and appetitive urges. In A. J. Elliot (Ed.), *Handbook of approach and avoidance motivation* (pp. 67–87). New York: Psychology Press.

Panksepp, J., & Solms, M. (2012). What is neuropsychoanalysis? Clinically relevant studies of the minded brain. *Trends in Cognitive Sciences, 16*, 6–8.

Paris, J. (2012). The rise and fall of dissociative identity disorder. *The Journal of Nervous and Mental Disease, 200*, 1076–1079.

Paris, J. (2019). Dissociative identity disorder: Validity and use in the criminal justice system. *BJPsych Advances, 25*, 287–293.

Passmore, J. A. (1935). The nature of intelligence. *Australasian Journal of Psychology and Philosophy, 13*, 279–289.

Passmore, J. (1961). *Philosophical reasoning*. London: Gerald Duckworth & Co.

Pataki, T. (1997). Self-deception and wish-fulfilment. *Philosophia, 25*, 297–322.

Pataki, T. (2000). Freudian wish-fulfilment & sub-intentional explanation. In M. P. Levine (Ed.), *The analytic Freud: Philosophy and psychoanalysis* (pp. 49–84). London: Routledge.

Pataki, T. (2014a). *Wishfulfilment in philosophy and psychoanalysis: The Tyranny of Desire*. London: Routledge.

Pataki, T. (2014b). Fairbairn and partitive conceptions of mind. In D. Scharff & G. Clarke (Eds.), *Fairbairn and the object relations tradition* (pp. 417–430). London: Karnac.

Pears, D. (1984). *Motivated irrationality*. Oxford: Clarendon Press.

Pears, D. (1986). The goals and strategies of self-deception. In J. Elster (Ed.), *The multiple self* (pp. 59–77). Cambridge: Cambridge University Press.

Petocz, A., & Newbery, G. (2010). On conceptual analysis as the primary qualitative approach to statistics education research in psychology. *Statistics Education Research Journal, 9*, 123–145.

Pica, M. (1999). The evolution of alter personality states in dissociative identity disorder. *Psychotherapy: Theory, Research, Practice, Training, 36*, 404–415.

Piper, A., & Merskey, H. (2004a). The persistence of folly: A critical examination of dissociative identity disorder. Part I. The excesses of an improbable concept. *The Canadian Journal of Psychiatry, 49*, 592–600.

Piper, A., & Merskey, H. (2004b). The persistence of folly: Critical examination of dissociative identity disorder. Part II. The defence and decline of multiple personality or dissociative identity disorder. *The Canadian Journal of Psychiatry, 49*, 678–683.

Prince, M. (1906). *The dissociation of a personality: A biographical study in abnormal psychology*. New York: Longmans, Green, and Company.

Pugh, G. (2002). Freud's 'problem': Cognitive neuroscience and psychoanalysis working together on memory. International Journal of Psychoanalysis, 83, 1375–1394.

Pugh, L. R., Taylor, P. J., & Berry, K. (2015). The role of guilt in the development of post-traumatic stress disorder: A systematic review. Journal of Affective Disorders, 182, 138–150.

Purcell, S. D. (2019). Psychic song and dance: Dissociation and duets in the analysis of trauma. *The Psychoanalytic Quarterly, 88*, 315–347.

Putnam, F. W. (1992). Discussion: Are alter personalities fragments or figments? *Psychoanalytic Inquiry, 12*, 95–111.

Raison, A., & Andrea, S. (2022). Childhood trauma in patients with dissociative identity disorder: A systematic review of data from 1990 to 2022: Psychotraumatisme dans l'enfance et survenue du trouble dissociatif de l'identité: une revue systématique des données publiées entre 1990 et 2022. *European Journal of Trauma & Dissociation, 7*, 100310.

Redgrave, P., Prescott, T. J., & Gurney, K. (1999). The basal ganglia: A vertebrate solution to the selection problem? *Neuroscience, 89*, 1000–1023.

Redgrave, P., Rodriguez, M., Smith, Y., Rodriguez-Oroz, M. C., Lehericy, S., Bergman, H., ... & Obeso, J. A. (2010). Goal-directed and habitual control in the basal ganglia: Implications for Parkinson's disease. *Nature Reviews Neuroscience, 11*, 760–772.

Reid, T. (1970). *Essays on the intellectual powers of man*. Menston: Scholar Press (Originally published 1785).

Reinders, A. S., Willemsen, A. T., Vos, H. P., den Boer, J. A., & Nijenhuis, E. R. (2012). Fact or factitious? A psychobiological study of authentic and simulated dissociative identity states. *PLoS One, 7*(6), e39279.

Reinders, A. A., & Veltman, D. J. (2021). Dissociative identity disorder: Out of the shadows at last? *The British Journal of Psychiatry, 219*, 413–414.

Richardson, M. J., Dale, R., & Marsh, K. L. (2014). Complex dynamical systems in social and personality psychology. In H. T. Reis & C. M. Judd (Eds.), *Handbook of research methods in social and personality psychology* (pp. 253–282). Cambridge: Cambridge University Press.

Ridderinkhof, V. K., Wildenberg, W. P. M., Segalowitz, S. J., & Carter, C. S. (2004). Neurocognitive mechanisms of cognitive control: The role of the prefrontal cortex in action selection, response inhibition, performance monitoring, and reward-based learning. *Brain & Cognition, 56*, 129–140.

Rofé, Y. (2008). Does repression exist? Memory, pathogenic, unconscious and clinical evidence. *Review of General Psychology, 12*, 63–85.

Rosenblatt, A. D., & Thickstun, J. T. (1977). Energy, information, and motivation: A revision of psycho-analytic theory. *Journal of the American Psycho-analytic Association, 25*, 537–558.

Ross, C. A. (2011). Possession experiences in dissociative identity disorder: A preliminary study. *Journal of Trauma & Dissociation, 12*, 393–400.

Ross, C. A. (2014). Unresolved problems in the theory of structural dissociation. *Psichiatria e Psicoterapia, 33*, 285–292.

Ross, C. (2022). False memory researchers misunderstand repression, dissociation and Freud. *Journal of Child Sexual Abuse, 31*, 488–502.

Ross, C., Schroeder, E., & Ness, L. (2014). Dissociation and symptoms of culture-bound syndromes in North America: A preliminary study. In V. Şar, W. Middleton, & M. Dorahy (Eds.), *Global perspectives on dissociative disorders:* Individual *and societal oppression* (pp. 87–98). London: Routledge.

Rychlak, J. E. (2000). Agency: An overview. In A. E. Kazdin (Ed.), *Encyclopedia of psychology* (pp. 102–104). Washington, DC: American Psychological Association.

Şar, V. (2014). The many faces of dissociation: Opportunities for innovative research in psychiatry. *Clinical Psychopharmacology and Neuroscience, 12*, 171–179.

Şar, V., Dorahy, M. J., & Krüger, C. (2017). Revisiting the etiological aspects of dissociative identity disorder: A biopsychosocial perspective. *Psychology Research and Behavior Management, 10*, 137–146.

Şar, V., & Ozturk, E. (2006). What is trauma and dissociation? *Journal of Trauma Practice, 4*, 7–20.

Sartre, J-.P. (1956). *Being and nothingness* (Translated by H. E. Barnes). New York: Philosophical Library.

Scarfone, D. (2021). Trauma, subjectivity and subjectality. *The American Journal of Psychoanalysis, 81*, 214–236.

Schauer, M., & Elbert, T. (2010). Dissociation following traumatic stress. *Zeitschrift für Psychologie/Journal of Psychology, 218*, 109–127.

Schimmenti, A. (2018). The trauma factor: Examining the relationships among different types of trauma, dissociation, and psychopathology. *Journal of Trauma & Dissociation, 19*, 552–571,

Schimmenti, A., & Caretti, V. (2016). Linking the overwhelming with the unbearable: Developmental trauma, dissociation, and the disconnected self. *Psychoanalytic Psychology, 33*, 106–128.

Schore, A. N. (2002). The neurobiology of attachment and early personality organization. *Journal of Prenatal and Perinatal Psychology and Health, 16*, 249–264.

Schore, A. N. (2009). Relational trauma and the developing right brain: An interface of psychoanalytic self psychology and neuroscience. *Annals of the New York Academy of Sciences, 1159,* 189–203.

Schreiber, F. R. (1973). *Sybil: The true story of a woman possessed by 16* separate *personalities.* Chicago: Regnery.

Searle, J. R. (1992). *The rediscovery of the mind.* Cambridge: MIT Press.

Searle, J. R. (2004). *Mind: A brief introduction.* Oxford: Oxford University Press.

Searle, J. R. (2005). The self as a problem in philosophy and neurobiology. In T. E. Feinberg & J. P. Keenan (Eds.), *The lost self: Pathologies of the brain and identity* (pp. 7–19). Oxford, New York: Oxford University Press.

Seligman, R., & Kirmayer, L. J. (2008). Dissociative experience and cultural neuroscience: Narrative, metaphor and mechanism. *Culture, Medicine & Psychiatry, 32,* 31–64.

Sermpezis, C., & Winter, D. A. (2009). Is trauma the product of over-or under-elaboration? A critique of the personal construct model of posttraumatic stress disorder. *Journal of Constructivist Psychology, 22,* 306–327.

Sleeth, D. B. (2006). The self and the integral interface: Toward a new understanding of the whole person. *The Humanistic Psychologist, 34,* 243–261.

Smit, H., & Hacker, P. M. (2014). Seven misconceptions about the mereological fallacy: A compilation for the perplexed. *Erkenntnis, 79,* 1077–1097.

Solms, M. (2013). The conscious id. *Neuropsychoanalysis, 15,* 5–19.

Solms, M. (2019). A neuropsychoanalytic perspective. *Psychoanalytic Inquiry, 39,* 607–624.

Solms, M. (2020). New project for a scientific psychology: General scheme. *Neuropsychoanalysis, 22,* 5–35.

Solms, M., & Panksepp, J. (2012). The "id" knows more than the "ego" admits: Neuropsychoanalytic and primal consciousness perspectives on the interface between affective and cognitive neuroscience. *Brain Science, 2,* 147–175.

Søndergaard, H. P. (2017). 'Janet vs Freud' on traumatization: A critique of the theory of structural dissociation from an object relations perspective. *British Journal of Psychotherapy, 33,* 418–421.

Song, J., Lin, H., & Liu, S. (2023). Basal ganglia network dynamics and function: Role of direct, indirect and hyper-direct pathways in action selection. *Network: Computation in Neural Systems, 34,* 84–121.

Smit, H., & Hacker, P. M. (2014). Seven misconceptions about the mereological fallacy: A compilation for the perplexed. *Erkenntnis, 79,* 1077–1097.

Spanos, N. P. (1994). Multiple identity enactments and multiple personality disorder: A sociocognitive perspective. *Psychological Bulletin, 116,* 143–165.

Spiegel, D. (2006). Recognizing traumatic dissociation. *American Journal of Psychiatry, 163,* 566–568.

Spiegel, D. (2010). Editorial: Dissociation in the DSM5. *Journal of Trauma & Dissociation, 11,* 261–265.

Spiegel, D., Lewis-Fernández, R., Lanius, R., Vermetten, E., Simeon, D., & Friedman, M. (2013). Dissociative disorders in DSM-5. *Annual Review of Clinical Psychology, 9,* 299–326.

Spiegel, D., Loewenstein, R. J., Lewis-Fernández, R., Sar, V., Simeon, D., Vermetten, E., Cardeña, E., & Dell, P. F. (2011). Dissociative disorders in DSM-5. *Depression and Anxiety, 2,* E17–E45.

Spiegel, R. (1986). Freud's refutation of degenerationism: A contribution to humanism. *Contemporary Psychoanalysis, 22,* 4–24.

Staniloiu, A., & Markowitsch, H. J. (2014). Dissociative amnesia. *The Lancet Psychiatry*, *1*, 226–241.

Steele, K. S., Dorahy, M. J., Van der Hart, O., & Nijenhuis, E. R. S. (2014a). Dissociation versus alterations in consciousness; related but different concepts. In P. F. Dell & J. A. O'Neil (Eds.), *In dissociation and the dissociative disorders: DSM-V and beyond* (pp. 155–170). New York: Routledge.

Steele, K. S., Van der Hart, O., & Nijenhuis, E. R. S. (2014b). The theory of trauma-related structural dissociation of the personality. In P. F. Dell & J. A. O'Neil (Eds.), *In dissociation and the dissociative disorders: DSM-V and beyond* (pp. 239–258). New York: Routledge.

Stephenson, C. (2015). The epistemological significance of possession entering the DSM. *History of Psychiatry*, *26*, 251–269.

Stern, D. B. (2009). Shall the twain meet? Metaphor, dissociation, and cooccurrence. *Psychoanalytic Inquiry*, *29*, 79–90.

Strohminger, N., Knobe, J., & Newman, G. (2017). The true self: A psychological concept distinct from the self. *Perspectives on Psychological Science*, *12*, 551–560.

Stuphorn, V. (2015). Neural mechanisms of response inhibition. *Current Opinion in Behavioral Sciences*, *1*, 64–71.

Stryker, S. (2008). From Mead to a structural symbolic interactionism and beyond. *Annual Review of Sociology*, *34*, 15–31.

Swanson, D. R. (1977). A critique of psychic energy as an explanatory concept. *Journal of the American Psychoanalytic Association*, *25*, 603–633.

Talvitie, V. (2009). *Freudian unconscious and cognitive neuroscience: From unconscious fantasies to neural algorithms*. London: Karnac.

Talvitie, V. (2012). *The foundations of psychoanalytic theories: Project for a scientific enough psychoanalysis*. London: Karnac.

Talvitie, V., & Ihanus, J. (2011). On neuropsychoanalytic metaphysics. *International Journal of Psychoanalysis*, *92*, 1583–1601.

Tarnopolsky, A. (2003). The concept of dissociation in early psychoanalytic writers. *Journal of Trauma & Dissociation*, *4*, 7–25.

Thelen, E., & Smith, L. B. (2007). Dynamic systems theories. In R. M. Lerner (Ed.), *Handbook of child psychology; Volume 1: Theoretical models of human development* (pp. 258–312). Hoboken, NJ: John Wiley & Sons, Inc.

Thompson, N. S. (1987). The misappropriation of teleonomy. In P. P. G. Bateson & P. H. Klopfer (Eds.), *Perspectives in ethology* (pp. 259–274). New York: Plenum.

Van der Hart, O., Nijenhuis, E., Steele, K., & Brown, D. (2004). Trauma-related dissociation: Conceptual clarity lost and found. *Australian & New Zealand Journal of Psychiatry*, *38*, 906–914.

Van der Hart, O., Van Dijke, A., Van Son, M., & Steele, K. (2001). Somatoform dissociation in traumatized World War I combat soldiers: A neglected clinical heritage. *Journal of Trauma & Dissociation*, *1*, 33–66.

Van der Hart, O. (2021). Trauma-related dissociation: An analysis of two conflicting models. *European Journal of Trauma & Dissociation*, *5*, 100210.

Van der Hart, O., & Dorahy, M. J. (2023). History of the concept of dissociation. In M. J. Dorahy, S. N. Gold & J. A. O'Neil (Eds.), *Dissociation and the dissociative disorders: past, present, future* (pp. 13–38). New York: Routledge.

Van der Hart, O., & Friedman, B. (2019). A reader's guide to Pierre Janet: A neglected intellectual heritage. In G. Craparo, F. Ortu, & O. Van der Hart (Eds.), *Rediscovering Pierre Janet: Trauma, dissociation, and a new context for psychoanalysis* (pp. 4–27). London: Routledge.

Van der Hart, O., & Horst, R. (1989). The dissociation theory of Pierre Janet. *Journal of Traumatic Stress, 2,* 397–412.

Van der Hart, O., Nijenhuis, E. R. S., & Steele, K. (2006). *The haunted self: Structural dissociation and the treatment of chronic traumatization.* New York: W. W. Norton & Co.

Van der Kolk, B. A. (1998). Trauma and memory. *Psychiatry and Clinical Neurosciences, 52*(S1), S52–S64.

Van der Kolk, B. A. (2000). Posttraumatic stress disorder and the nature of trauma. *Dialogues in Clinical Neuroscience, 2,* 7–22.

Van der Kolk, B. A. (2003). Psychobiology of posttraumatic stress disorder. In J. Panksepp (Ed.), *Textbook of biological psychiatry* (pp. 319–344). Hoboken, NJ: John Wiley & Sons.

Van der Kolk, B. A. (2005). Developmental trauma disorder: Toward a rational diagnosis for children with complex trauma histories. *Psychiatric Annals, 35,* 401–408.

Van der Kolk, B. A., & Fisler, R. (1995). Dissociation and the fragmentary nature of traumatic memories: Overview and exploratory study. *Journal of Traumatic Stress, 8,* 505–525.

Van der Kolk, B. A., Herron, N., & Hostetler, A. (1994). The history of trauma in psychiatry. *Psychiatric Clinics of North America, 17,* 583–600.

Van der Kolk, B. A., & McFarlane, A. C. (1996). The black hole of trauma. In B. A. Van der Kolk, A. C. McFarlane, & L. Weisaeth (Eds.), *Traumatic stress; The effects o overwhelming experience on mind, body, and society* (pp. 3–23). New York: Guildford.

Van Inwagen, P., & Zimmerman, D. W. (2008). Introduction: What is metaphysics? In P. van Inwagen & D. W. Zimmerman (Eds.), *Metaphysics: The big questions* (pp. 1–14). Malden, MA: Blackwell.

Wakefield, J. C. (2007). The concept of mental disorder: Diagnostic implications of the harmful dysfunction analysis. *World Psychiatry, 6,* 149–156.

Waelder, R. (1960). *Basic theory of psychoanalysis.* New York: International Universities Press.

Watkins, H. H. (1993). Ego-state therapy: An overview. *American Journal of Clinical Hypnosis, 35,* 232–240.

Watson, J. B., & Rayner, R. (1920). Conditioned emotional reactions. *Journal of Experimental Psychology, 3,* 1–14. (Reprinted in 2000 in *American Psychologist, 55,* 313–317).

Wegner, D. M. (2005). Who is the controller of controlled processes? In R. R. Hassin, J. S. Uleman, & J. A. Bargh (Eds.), *The new unconscious* (pp. 19–36). Oxford: Oxford University Press.

Wegner, D. M., & Wheatley, T. (1999). Apparent mental causation: Sources of the experience of will. *American Psychologist, 54,* 480–492.

White, P. A. (1990). Ideas about causation in philosophy and psychology. *Psychological Bulletin, 108,* 3–18.

Whitmer, G. (2001). On the nature of dissociation. *The Psychoanalytic Quarterly, 70,* 807–837.

Wilkie, I. C., Dolan, S., Lewis, J., & Blake, D. R. (2007). 'Autotomy': A terminological inexactitude. *Pain, 128,* 286–287.

Williams, R. A. (2018). Lessons learned on development and application of agent-based models of complex dynamical systems. *Simulation Modelling Practice and Theory, 83,* 201–212.

Wilson, J. P. (2007). The lens of culture: Theoretical and conceptual perspectives in the assessment of psychological trausma and PTSD. In J. P. Wilson & C. S. Tang (Eds.),

Cross-cultural assessment of psychological trauma and PTSD (pp. 3–30). Boston, MA: Springer US.

Wise, R. A. (2004). Drive, incentive, and reinforcement: The antecedents and consequences of motivation. In R. Dienstbier, R. A. Bevins, & M. T. Bardo (Eds.), *Motivational factors in the etiology of drug abuse: Volume 50 of the Nebraska symposium on motivation* (pp. 159–195). Lincoln: University of Nebraska Press.

Wright, J. S., & Panksepp, J. (2012). An evolutionary framework to understand foraging, wanting, and desire: The neuropsychology of the SEEKING system. *Neuropsychoanalysis, 14*, 5–39.

Zachar, P. (2000). Psychiatric disorders are not natural kinds. *Philosophy, Psychiatry, & Psychology, 7*, 167–182.

Zepf, S. (2001). Incentives for a reconsideration of the debate on metapsychology. *International Journal of Psychoanalysis, 82*, 463–482.

Zepf, S., & Zepf, F. D. (2008). Trauma and traumatic neurosis: Freud's concepts revisited. *The International Journal of Psychoanalysis, 89*, 331–353.

Index

For Product Safety Concerns and Information please contact our EU
representative GPSR@taylorandfrancis.com
Taylor & Francis Verlag GmbH, Kaufingerstraße 24, 80331 München, Germany

9 780367 428976